A Father Losing His Daughter to Addiction

By

Anthony M. Varone

DORRANCE PUBLISHING CO
EST. 1920
PITTSBURGH, PENNSYLVANIA 15238

Dorrance Publishing Co
585 Alpha Drive
Pittsburgh, PA 15238
Visit our website at www.dorrancebookstore.com

ISBN: 979-8-88812-226-6
eISBN: 979-8-88812-726-1

This book is dedicated to my daughter, Laura Nicole Varone; to all those who are currently dealing with addiction; and to all those who have felt hopeless and have lost their way and their faith in both themselves and God. I hope this book can help, educate, and heal all those who have loved ones who are dealing with addiction, or the addicts themselves.

The Beginning

My daughter Laura Nicole Varone was born on January 24, 1995, at 12:40 PM at Princeton Medical Center in Princeton, N.J. It was a typical cold day in January with snow flurries. I remember that day as I watched the doctor deliver her to this brand-new world that awaited her.

She was perfect in every way and so beautiful. I remember saying to myself that she is mine and thanking God for this perfect miracle.

I always wanted a daughter in my life to give her all the things I had not had—especially a good education and good schools—and I wanted to provide a safe, loving home, just as my parents provided for me. I clearly remember driving her home with my wife and saying that I would die for my daughter. I remember this as if it was yesterday. She would always come first in my life.

I was so happy and proud to be a father, but I was especially proud to be her father. I knew I would love her unconditionally, just as my mom loved me. I would lead by my mother's example. I would take this responsibility very seriously and be the father she deserved and would need in her life and in life itself. I would protect her, love her, and always be there for her no matter what. I would make her feel special and wanted every day. I would encourage her to be her best and do her best and believe in herself, just as my parents believed in me when I was growing up. I would try to be a great mentor and try not to judge her. I would raise her Catholic and have her exposed to God. I felt this was so important, since so many children have little or no values or beliefs in religion. Also, I would make sure that I would never hit her when she did something wrong, for I knew this was wrong, and it was how my father punished me and all my siblings. I didn't want to carry this dysfunction in my life in raising my daughter.

Laura had all the expectancies of a newborn, so tiny and yet so precious. She slept well and ate well each day. She was growing up so fast and beginning to crawl by seven months. She was a perfect joy and a happy, healthy, beautiful little baby girl.

We gave her all our love and attention with each day that God allowed us to be united with her. And yes, you could say we made her our whole life and spoiled her, but I always say we spoiled her with love, not material things. Again, it's what my mom gave me: love always.

My wife stayed home with her for the first year, as her job allowed her this, for which we were very grateful. We felt this was important and it would form a special bond between mother and daughter. I always wish my wife could have just stayed home until Laura was ready for school, but I know she would have lost her job if she did that, and we really needed her income at the time. Now, looking back, I know we would have been better to lose the job rather than lose that time with Laura.

A stay-at-home mom makes such a difference to both the child and the family. My mom was always home: She never worked except for housework and raising her children, which is a very difficult job. I came from a family of five siblings. Having her home each day really made a difference growing up. I remember all the unconditional love she would always give us; not to mention the strict upbringing as well. When I look back at those times, they were priceless, and they really helped me and my siblings grow up to be respectful, responsible, and obedient. There wasn't much you could get away with, having a stay-at-home mom , so it really did pay off, and through the years, I always saw that with my friends whose moms were busy working and not home to see the mischief and trouble their children would get into. I would still say, even today, you can always spot a stay-at-home mom's child.

Knowing what I know now, I would have done anything to have Laura protected and guided in those early years, even if it meant me staying home to raise her. Laura was worth it and so much more. But here again, not every mom can stay home; both mentally and financially, it has to be right for the mom.

Laura, unfortunately, was not exposed to much family when she was an infant. My mother was diagnosed with dementia, and my father was already in a nursing home with Alzheimer's. My father never even met her or knew of her, ever. It always saddened me that my parents were not able to be a part of Laura's life because I know my mom would have spoiled her with love and affection. She would have been a great influence on her and in her life. She would have been firm but given her nothing but unconditional love, just as she always gave me.

Plus, she would have helped me with all her experience in raising five children. And oh, how I needed the help and would need the help. Here I was, trying my best to raise the daughter of my dreams, along with my wife, who was dealing with her own problem: addiction. My wife was an alcoholic and had only been sober for a year before Laura was born. I never knew she had a problem because I was very naïve, and I came from an Italian family with no addictions whatsoever. I had no experience in spotting, nor did I have the knowledge to spot, someone who has addiction issues, so this was very difficult for me. And little did I know that Laura had a 50 percent chance of having addictions herself in life. I learned this later in the years to come.

My wife's parents also suffered with addiction. Even though her father was also in recovery, it was still hard for everyone, and they really couldn't be involved with Laura as much as they would like, or with us for that matter.

My wife's mom was far away and had health issues as well. She passed away shortly after Laura was born. I never knew much about addiction since I was never exposed to it and never really had friends or family who were suffering with addiction. I came from a family of immigrants, and they never really drank. My father would make his own wine, as most Italians did, both here and in Italy. He would have a small glass with his dinner each night but never, ever abused it. My mother never touched alcohol. We always did have alcohol in the house, but it was mainly for when company came over to visit. It's always an Italian tradition to put out different liquors, wine, and lots of food. None of my siblings ever drank; we just didn't have a likening for it or see the appeal of it, and so we never needed it in our lives. We felt it was not our thing . I would drink sometimes with my friends as I was growing up, but I never had more than two drinks of any alcohol. I really never needed or had any desire to party like everyone else my age was doing. I did experiment with mairjuana and Quaaludes, but again, I never wanted more of it but to try it.

I was very lucky coming from an immigrant family that had no addictions, not even in our family tree or our bloodline. We had so many cousins and relatives, both here and in Italy, and here again, no one had issues with addiction. Even when my parents spoke, I never remember them speaking about a relative, or anyone, who had problems dealing with addiction. My family was always known for their hard work and making their family a priority. It was never about partying with alcohol and cigarettes, as I saw so much of it growing up with my friends and their parents. I remember my parents always saying that's the "Americans""; that's "their way."

I remember always trying to instill good values in my daughter as she was growing up. Everything that was passed on to me or learned from my parents, I tried to give back and teach to her. I felt this was really important and would lay the groundwork for a good, firm future.

Growing up, we were raised Roman Catholic; that, of course, was a result of our parents coming from Italy. We had Laura baptized and had her make her Holy Communion. We tried to install God in her life, and church , but things changed once my wife and I got divorced. It was difficult now to bring her up by us not going to church as a family. This is very common when there is divorce and the child is young or too young to have a strong belief in religion or some kind of higher power. I always tried to talk positive about God and how He would help us and her if we prayed to Him. I wanted Laura to know that I believed, and I wanted her to know she should believe and pray also because God would always be there for her as long as she spoke to Him and trusted Him to help her whenever she needed His help, love, and guidance.

As my wife returned to work, we were able to use a very close friend of my sister's to watch Laura while we were at work. I was happy about that because I had known my sister's friend Carol since I was young, so I knew Laura was in good hands and would be treated well and would be cared for; something that was very important to me as well as my wife. Too many times, we would hear of children being abused or neglected. I didn't want to have to worry about that.

I was so worried about Laura from day one, and that's how it was always for me when it came to Laura. I just couldn't turn off the worrying, something I picked up from my mom. My mom couldn't turn off the worrying when it came to her children, and that's what we were shown—not that it was a good thing; but I guess that's what the love of your children does to you. And boy did I know this too well already. I knew it was not healthy to be this way, and I also knew I would have to work on this.

From an early age, we started taking Laura to the beach, and from day one, she loved it, just as I did. My parents used to take us to the shore all the time, especially to Wildwood in New Jersey to visit our cousins who had several businesses on the boardwalk. I always loved the beach and, of course, summertime. We always had the best of times at the beach with all my family, and I wanted Laura to enjoy it all as much as I always did. Laura used to love playing in the sand for hours on end, and I would be there with her, helping her build sandcastles and the moat that we would fill with the water from the waves. Once high tide came in, it would destroy the castle and its moat. I always remember how sad she would get when the water ran over all of her hard work, and I would always tell her not to worry because we could always build more the next time we came down. Her mom and I even bought her a sandbox with a lid for our backyard, so she could play in it and use it anytime she wanted.

Later in life, Laura would be looking for that beach life, but in a different way. All this will be told and explained later in this book.

Laura was then put into preschool at the age of three-and-a-half. That was very difficult for both her and us. She would cry every day when we dropped her off, and I hated each day that she cried; it just broke my heart. I remember getting to work and calling them to see how she was. It was so hard having an only child because they become your whole world, unlike when you have more than one; it can't be that way, nor should it. My mom always said it's not good to just have one; you need to have several children. And it was so true. I did, however, find that out quick.

My wife and I found ourselves going through a divorce when Laura was four years old. We struggled from day one of our marriage, and me dealing with her addiction to alcohol was just something that I couldn't deal with, nor did I want to. It was so stressful having a wife with addiction, and I didn't know how to cope with it or find peace with it. And even though I knew that divorce was wrong and not accepted in the Catholic religion, I still wanted out. After 13 years of marriage, I knew I couldn't do any more. I was spent.

My wife was able to get me an annulment from the Catholic Church since I married under false pretense due to the fact that she wasn't truly honest about her drinking and addiction. I was grateful to her for doing that because now I could get married in a Catholic church again if I so desired.

Laura did well in preschool, and before we knew it, she was

graduating even though her parents were now divorced. She was still too young to understand what divorce was and why it happened to her parents.

Although we were divorced, we agreed to make Laura always a priority and to show her that we loved her even though we were no longer married. My now ex-wife and I also had a mutual agreement to not show Laura our differences and to show that we were still a family even though we were divorced. I always wanted Laura to know the divorce had nothing to do with her even though I felt guilty about the divorce itself. I had always wished it didn't have to be that way, and that our marriage would have survived. I had always believed that many broken children come from broken or divorced marriages. I never really wanted to divorce my wife, but I knew I couldn't live this kind of life; a life filled with addiction and misery. Not everyone can handle addiction or have a spouse who has and suffers with addiction. That isn't to say that I was perfect or came with no faults. No; not at all. It is best to say that we needed our separate lives ; and, of course, what would be best for Laura and her future.

Laura was now five and entering kindergarten. She had some friends already who would be in the same school as her. Her mom lived in the town that was close to her school, and I lived in the next town over. Our homes were close to each other's, so traveling back and forth between the two homes wasn't ever a problem. I had Laura several times a week as well as on the weekends. I didn't want to have that every other week schedule as most couples have who get divorced. I felt it was important to see her and share her as much as possible. I wanted to be involved with all aspects of her life, both now and in the future.

It really bothered me, and I hated the fact that I couldn't say goodnight to her every night. I always remember growing up and having both my parents there when I went to bed. It's what every child 'needs, and probably wants. It's what I always called a "normal" childhood life to be with both parents both in the morning and going to bed at night. I remember crying many nights because I couldn't see my daughter go to bed each night, especially in the beginning stage of the divorce. It was a difficult time of my life and a big adjustment all the way around. It was also difficult playing both mom and dad to Laura, filling in where needed for both parents. Again, here is something that I never experienced because my parents were always home and living under the same roof , so if my mom needed to talk to my father, she knew he was always there or would be home later to discuss whatever was needed for whatever child.

My parents were now both in specialized care for their dementia and Alzheimer's. As I said earlier, my dad never knew or met my daughter. He didn't even know me or the rest of my siblings. His Alzheimer's had progressed to that. I really couldn't believe this was happening to them both, me, and my siblings. That really saddened me knowing that my parents could never enjoy Laura or help me raise her. I always wanted my mom to be there for Laura. Every child should have grandparents to spoil them and love them , and I had always wanted that for Laura, but God had other plans for my parents —plans that I didn't like or even understand. I am glad that my mom got to spend some time with Laura before she got to where she didn't know her or remember her anymore. I would take my mom out to lunch and bring Laura with me even though my mom was not well and Laura was just five at the time. I wanted Laura to remember her grandmom (her Nonna) even though she was not well. I felt this was important for Laura to be around her, even if my mom didn't have long to live. I had hoped that she would remember my mom as she got older and would remember the goodness and love in her. I never got to meet my mom's parents and only saw my dad's father twice. My grandparents lived in both Italy and Argentina and had passed while I was young. I always wanted to meet them, especially my grandparents on my mom's side. I had always heard such nice things about them, plus I knew my mom loved them so much, especially her father, who I was named after. I felt so bad for my mom: She came to this country from Italy with no family; she was all alone. My dad had relatives here, and his brothers also came to live in the U.S. after he was here for several years. But my mom had given up everything and everyone once she left Italy. I know that had to be so hard for her and my sadness was for her always, and always would be.

Laura always needed attention growing up; she was used to being the only child, so doing things by herself or accompanying her, time alone was not easy for her. She would always ask me, "What are we going to be doing now?" or "What should I do next, Daddy?" That was not easy, nor did I ever get used to that. It caused panic and anxiety for me. I always found myself looking for things to do for her or ways to keep her busy while I tried to get things I needed done in the house or for myself. I would schedule play dates to keep her amused or accompanied. I really didn't know what else to do or how to handle this. I was like a fish out of water or in an area that I had no experience with.

Luckily, I now had met someone very special; her name was Helen, and she also was divorced and had a daughter of her own. Even though her daughter was 10 years older than Laura, she still was a mom with all that experience of raising a daughter. I am extremely grateful she was always there to help me and Laura. Helen was an excellent mom and had the patience of a saint. There were days I wouldn't have known what to do if I didn't have her help or couldn't reach out to her. She was great with Laura and cared for her very much.

Laura was very comfortable being with Helen and being around her. Helen's daughter Jackie was also helpful with Laura and the two got along well with each other. Helen would many times take Laura out, so I could get things done. She would even take Laura to her friends who also had children, so Laura could be with other children to play or go places. Helen would many times take Laura to get her nails done or a pedicure. Laura really liked that because it made her feel like a queen and made her feel very special. I truly appreciate all Helen did for Laura and the time she spent with her.

I was lost many times with Laura, and it wasn't easy as a father having a girl to guide, watch over, and raise even though I had the help of Helen and Laura's mom. Everyone always said to me it would be easier if I had a boy rather than a girl. I have always said, "I'm blessed to have a beautiful girl, and I wouldn't trade it for the world."

I felt many times that I was in way over my head while raising Laura, being a divorced dad with a child who was a girl. I never complained about my situation; I guess I was just scared and didn't ever know what to expect with all this or how things would play out. I still had my siblings also, who were always there for me and who supported me with everything I was going through and dealing with. My twin brother was Laura's godfather when she was baptized. He was very generous to Laura, both at Christmas time and for her birthday, and would buy her such expensive gifts. He always treated Laura like she was his own daughter, and he loved her dearly. You could always see it in Laura. She always respected him and loved him as well. Joseph and I are twins, and I think Laura always had that connection to him because he was a part of me. I always loved seeing that Laura really liked when he was around and loved to be with him. I'm very fortunate to have a great twin brother like him, and I thank my mom and God for this.

I always felt close to my twin but could never share with him about my marriage, especially that I married an addict. I felt totally embarrassed to tell my family about my problems and all I was dealing with while my wife was an alcoholic. I really should have trusted them with my unhappiness and problems I was having , and now, looking back, I know I made so many mistakes and should have confided in them. I know they wouldn't have judged me; they would have supported me.

We signed Laura up for swimming because neither of us could really swim well, and we felt it was important for her to know how to swim. I was living in a community that had several pools, and I would be taking her to the pool each summer along with going to the shore, so having her know how to swim would be helpful and keep her safe. Laura did really well and learned fast with her swimming lessons. She loved the pool and, of course, the beach.

I decided that following year to buy Laura a hamster for her birthday. We had already a small miniature poodle named Noah from my marriage to her mom. But Laura wasn't that crazy about Noah because he was just a dog. Not that she didn't love him, because she did; she loved animals in general, but she wanted her own hamster. We ended up going to PetSmart, and I had her pick out her own hamster. She was just so happy and excited to have a hamster that she picked the name Hammy. I thought that was so cute yet clever of her to come up with this adorable name for her pet hamster. She absolutely loved having this hamster and would hold him and hug him all the time. Problem was, she didn't really clean up after him or clean out his cage. That was a job that I got stuck with. I felt so bad for her as always because she was between two houses all the time, going back and forth, so I ended up always doing it for her. And yes, I was not setting a good example or being strict enough when it came to Laura. I always knew this and was very weak in so many ways when it came to her and the divorce, her mom having problems and in recovery, etc. The list went on and on. I guess I was a dream come true for therapy or a therapist.

It was so funny to see Laura take Hammy out for a walk. She had him on a little piece of string that she would walk him on. She would even teach him tricks…or least, she would try to teach him tricks. She was very attached to her hamster, and when she was at her mom's house, she would always ask me how he was and if I was taking good care of him. I was always hoping to teach her responsibility with her hamster along with many other things. I felt it was important that she know to take care of him and not neglect her pet hamster that she wanted so bad.

For the time that Hammy was alive, Laura did love him and enjoyed her time with him. The problem was that hamsters don't live long, and after eight months, he ended up dying. I got her another one, but after some time, that one also died, and at this point, Laura had pretty much outgrown of wanting any-more hamsters. Here again, she was always so quick to move on to the next thing or just lose interest. Staying in the moment and enjoying where she was, was just so very hard for her.

Laura was very bright and picked up fast in everything she applied herself to. Her teachers always had great things to say about her and would share with us all the positive things about her. The only negative comment or concern would be that she would rush to finish her work rather than taking her time and rechecking her work. She would have had perfect papers and assignments had she had taken her time. We started noticing that in everything she did'. It was as if she just wanted to get it done and not stay in the moment. As time went on and she got older, she had a hard time in staying in the moment and not rushing. No matter how much she was told or reminded by us to slow down, she continued with trying to finish quickly. Her school and teachers never mentioned anything as far as a learning disability or an attention deficit disorder. Her grades were always good but could have been perfect had she slowed down, so her mom and I just accepted this about her and felt this was who she was and never really tried to change her.

At around age 10, Laura's mom moved to the same town where I was living, and Laura would now go to the schools in our community. It made it so that we could now have her close to both of our homes and her in the same school district as where we were living. I was glad for that because it was a much better school district compared to where she started kindergarten, and I wanted Laura to be in the best schools possible. I attended schools that were not really the best when it came to learning. Even though it's not the schools you go to but what you make of it, I just wanted Laura always to have better and the best education.

By age 11, we had signed up Laura for gymnastics and dance. We wanted her to be involved in activities that would keep her busy as well as expose her to all the different activities and sports there were. And, of course, we wanted her to have fun and learn from these, so she could see what interested her. Laura was always good at everything she tried but wasn't always interested in pursuing it or giving it her best. It was more like just doing it to do it, but her heart wasn't into it. I noticed that with school and all the other things she would try or do. I wanted Laura to have something she loved and was passionate about; something that made her say, "I really want this and will give it my all." I always told Laura that it was important to have fun with what you wanted to pursue or follow. Being good at something is great, but enjoying it also is very important.

The following summer, Helen and I decided to take a vacation to Disney World in Florida and take Laura with us. It would also be my first time to Florida and Disney World. I fell in love with Florida, its weather, and all the beauty it had to offer. I was especially in love with all the flowers that were always in bloom and the beautiful palm trees that were everywhere the eye could see.

We took Laura to Magic Kingdom on our second day in Florida but found it to be overwhelming to say the least. Laura didn't really want to stay long at the park and wanted to go back to the hotel and enjoy the pool, so unfortunately, our day was cut short at the park and didn't go according to our plan. I know I probably should have just made her stay there and deal with it since we spent so much money on the tickets, but I gave in to her, and we left to go back to the pool at the hotel. To be totally honest, I too was having a problem with all of it, so I was okay with going back to the hotel. I think it was too much too soon, and the two of us were not ready for all we had to see and do at this huge, overwhelming park. I'm not trying to make an excuse for Laura, but I was also trying always to please her for several reasons:

one being I always felt guilty about the divorce; and the other that I was codependent of Laura and her life. I was up and feeling good only when she was happy and feeling good. When she was down or unhappy and sad, I too was feeling that way. Not a good way to be, and not very healthy to say the least for me. I was aware of this problem for a long time and also was told about it from my therapist—not that I needed to be told because I had already learned this about myself with Laura.

Signs of co-dependency are the desire to fix or save people and feel needed; putting others' needs before your own; having problems with confrontation as well as decision making; and doing whatever it takes to keep a relationship together.

This was all me when it came to Laura, and I knew it wasn't a good thing nor could I live with it. It also wasn't good for Laura to see this because it would make her know that I lived for her and whatever she wanted, she could have or use it to control me.

I had my work cut out for me, and here I again, easier said than done. Not an easy fix for me by any means at all.

Through the years, Laura made friends both at school and outside of school. She never had a lot of friends but would always be close to one. She would surround herself with that one friend, and when that one friend wasn't around or available, she found herself lost. She wouldn't know what to do with herself'. It's as if she became dependent on that friend. We always tried to teach her not become so attached to one friend; that way, she wouldn't feel down or left out if that friend was unavailable. I would always encourage her to have a lot of friends—"The more, the merrier!" I would tell her. But unfortunately, that never really happened.

As Laura got older, we started to notice her not having the confidence she should have. She couldn't be around those who were prettier than her or smarter. Laura felt very uncomfortable when she had friends who were more popular or prettier. Again, I think it was a low self-esteem she developed as she got older, and it just continued to get worse.

We had Laura enrolled in the before- and after-care for school since we both were working and couldn't change our hours to that of school. I always felt bad for Laura since she couldn't just be at school the hours required. But we had no other choice than the before- and after-care. It wasn't as if she was the only one there enrolled in the program. Her regular friends were not in the aftercare, but she did make friends; just not close friends. I know she never really liked it because it made it a very long day. And for that, I felt for her. I had my mom home, as I mentioned before so when school was out, we walked home. In those days, all moms were home, unlike today when almost all moms have to work and also have careers as well. Plus, today, you have so many single moms juggling their careers and children at the same time. I had always wondered if Laura resented us for having her in the before- and after-care program. I know I shouldn't look back at that, but I always do. So many things I just wish I could have changed when it came to Laura. But I have to keep reminding myself that I did the best I could at the time and leave it at that. Otherwise, it will consume me, as so much of it does till this day.

As the years went by Laura began to act out and become her own person with her own personality. She would always be trying to draw attention to herself both by the way she acted and dressed. She wanted to be noticed and to stand out from the rest. We watched her closely because she wanted things her way and not ours. It seemed like she was a calling out for help, or was saying, "Look at me and let's see what I can get away with." She was now in the teenage years and wanted a cell phone. We felt she wasn't ready for that, plus there was the fear we had with the internet and texting. It was a constant battle that we had with her about having a phone and all the responsibility that goes with it. Most of her friends had cell phones, especially her closest friend. But unlike her friends, we just felt that Laura wasn't ready for that, nor were we. We would see her sometimes using her friends' phone to text others, which we knew it was most likely boys. Laura had developed an attention-craving behavior, especially coming from boys , which is something we couldn't understand because she always had our attention and love. As her father, I gave her nothing but my full attention, always.

But that's not what she wanted; she wanted that approval of the boys. She wanted a boy or boys to love her and make it all about her. She didn't like it when her friends got more attention than her when it came to boys. It was now that Laura saw girls as being the enemy instead of boys. She didn't like it when there were girls who were prettier than her or more popular than her: This was competition, and she wasn't comfortable with that. She didn't want to deal with that or have that in her life.

We were very concerned about all this; it's as if we saw the red flags go up, but we didn't know what to do. We saw this as not normal behavior for our daughter, or any daughter for that matter. My ex-wife found herself talking to her friends and asking what they were experiencing with their children. She also did some research and started to read up about teenager behavior.

As time went by, Laura got worse with all of this, she now began to sneak out at night to be with her friends, but mostly, it was to be with boys. Laura had now developed or had oppositional defiant disorder (ODD), which consists of anger, irritability, arguing, defiance, or vindictiveness. It's a behavior that is learned sometimes. We started taking her to a psychologist who specialized in children with behavioral problems, including ODD. We were desperate for help and as well as scared for our daughter; we knew nothing of this or how bad it could be or get. I was the one who usually would take Laura due to my ex-wife having her own issues and problems she was dealing with. I would sometimes sit in on the sessions with Laura and talk about my concerns or what I saw with her and how she was dealing or coping with everything. I just wanted Laura to be normal and not have to deal or suffer with any of this. I really wanted her to enjoy her teenager years and have fun, both in school and out of school.

We also started to see her grades drop off and her not being interested in school whatsoever. She even started to talk about quitting school, and that just really got to me. I hated school myself but never thought about dropping out nor was it an option with my parents. They would have killed me; especially my father. He would never stand for that. Both of my parents had no education or ever attended school, I was glad that I had that fear of my parents because I know they had my best interest in mind, and I definitely needed direction growing up.

Looking back now at Laura and what she was going through at that time, we realize she was dealing with major anxiety as well as behavioral problems. Having anxiety and not being able to cope with what is normal to others makes it very difficult to be positive about anything or have the desire to succeed in life. Her mom had to deal with anxiety as well in her life, and that's one of the reasons she would self-medicate with alcohol; to relieve that anxiety that would rule her life.

Both me and her mom were trying to help Laura before bigger problems arose. We wanted to educate her, as well as ourselves, so we would all be on the same page as a family even though we were divorced. We just wanted to help Laura and had her best interest at mind.

Every day was scary with Laura. We never know what she would do or what she was feeling. She really didn't open up to us much. We know one of the issues was not having a cell phone, and that was also told to us by her therapist. We also found out that Laura had stolen an Apple iPod Touch from a gym locker in school. She did this, so she would have internet access to be on MySpace, a social website which started back in 2005 and was like Facebook, which is very popular now. We were so upset when we found this out that, we ended taking her to the police and telling them what she did in hopes that it would scare her to never think about doing that again. But when we did take her to the police, she wasn't affected by any of it; it was like she was numb to it all or she didn't think it was a big deal. Laura was living in her own world and justifying her actions due to what she wanted or what she was dealing with.

There were many factors involved with Laura and her behavior. We knew this better than anyone since we were her parents. But the problem was, we didn't know how to help her. We couldn't fix what went bad or what was breaking inside of her, and as a parent, that is a horrible feeling since all you want to do is help your child or get them the help they need so desperately.

I kept taking Laura to her therapist in hopes that she would help her as well as us. I was really glad that Laura connected with her and was willing to go to her because most children are in denial and blame everything on their parents or the world when it comes to their problems. Not to stay that Laura wasn't like that, because she was. Most of the time, she never took ownership of anything she did wrong, even when she got into trouble. It was another one of her problems that seemed to be getting worse. Whether it was school, friends or her life with us, or just everyday things, lying and manipulating was one of her specialties now. It came down to where we never knew if she was telling the truth, and every situation, happening, or event had to be checked or double-checked to see if that was really the truth. If she was going out with her friend, it could be a lie to be with a boy or doing something she shouldn't be doing. Or the famous one of where she was with a girlfriend, but only to leave the house and later meet with a boy. It became so frustrating and upsetting to deal with all this and to know what she was doing. It really wasn't her fault she had these behavioral problems. No one wants these types of personality or behavioral problems; it's something that we are given, learn, or both. And if they are not identified or controlled, they can lead to bigger problems down the road or later in life. That was always our fear with Laura, knowing that bigger problems or more serious issues could be happening or developing. As Laura got older it seems her self-esteem had disappeared; she had very little confidence in herself or her goals. Many girls, especially pretty girls, have low self-esteem, and Laura was definitely one of those girls, so very pretty, yet she felt like she lacked all of it: looks, intelligence, and confidence. I never understood that about Laura—how she had everything, being attractive, smart, and outgoing—yet she had nothing. It's as if she was just a shell and empty on the inside. I was always average all my life, and here I had a daughter who was so above average in everything, but she could never see that about herself. And she didn't believe it if you told her or believe in herself. This was so upsetting to see her struggle with all this. Again, I felt so hopeless every time a new problem would take on Laura. I just wanted to fix her and take it all away for her, but I know I couldn't. So many therapists would say in my readings that each child has all the tools they need to help themselves, and that's what they said about Laura. But that wasn't the case here; Laura was not equipped with the tools or the know-how on how to fix her own problems. Each child is different and is not textbook material, as many therapists label them as. You can't group them or lump them all together. That's only in a perfect world; and we don't live in a perfect world, and neither do our children—especially today with all the problems and the issues they face each day. It's not like it was when I was growing up 40-plus years ago; we could always handle our own issues or problems by ourselves. And when we couldn't, we looked to our parents and family for help, not our friends.

Today, most kids go to their friends or social media for help with their problems. They put it out there for everyone to see or vent it through their social media accounts. This is a much different world we now live in. It's like whatever you need, you can go to the web for help or advice or express your anger to those who will listen to you. But that can be dangerous also because you don't know who may be giving you advice, and if you can trust them or even know who they are.

I knew Laura was putting herself out there, and that really scared me. I had no control of what she was putting out there or looking at. As I said, she was very good at making it look like she wasn't doing anything because she didn't have a cell phone, but I knew she was using her friends' phones or using them to get what she needed. I never liked that she would just use someone for what they had or to get her needs met. I felt we raised her to be better than that, but then again, it's as if I didn't know who she was or who she was becoming... It was very upsetting.

I prayed each day when Laura was born and gave thanks to the Lord our God for the greatest miracle He gave us. And as things got worse with Laura, I prayed He would help her as well as us and show us the way. I felt God would always be there for her, as He was always there for me. Problem was, I just didn't know God's plan or how this would all play out.

As Laura turned 15, we broke down and got her a cell phone; not that we wanted to, but we thought that the peer pressure of not having one was taking its toll on her, as well as us trying to deal with all of this and her hating us for not allowing her to have one. I knew this was going to be difficult and a real challenge for us. We tried to instill in her how important it was to have a cell phone and how she needed to be careful with it and how she used it. We knew this would just be like, "Yes I know," and "Yes, you told me that already..." may be the norm for most teenagers, but not the norm for Laura. I knew we had our work cut out for us, and every day, we had to watch her and stay on top of her with the cell phone and how she was using it. Even her therapist suggested giving Laura some responsibility and trust when using her cell phone. Her therapist always said that children as well as teenagers need choices, so they feel they have a part in their own lives, and it's not just dictated from their parents.

And I totally agree. My parents always told me what to do, and I didn't have a choice in the matter or decision. I hated that, but that's the way it was with them. Children need choices. to give them a value and make them feel good about themselves. Even if it's a bad choice, it's how they learn; and hopefully, they learn from their mistakes.

As time went by, we found out things about how Laura was using her cell phone and how it became an obsession. It was like nothing else mattered but being with her cell phone or having it with her at all times. We would tell her that the cell phone needed to be limited and not be with her constantly. We made sure that she didn't have it when we ate dinner; there had to be rules. We knew this all would be difficult, and was a trying time for us.

We also were now dealing with Laura as I stated before Laura continued to be sneaking out—and it wasn't through the front door but through her bedroom window. This was very disturbing to say the least. Only God knows what kind of trouble she could get into or what she was up to. We now were constantly checking on her when she was in her room and sleeping to make sure she was still there. She somehow managed to remove the screen from the window and jump down off the roof of her mom's home. She would usually sneak out from her mom's home since the roof was lower, and it was easier to do without getting hurt. I couldn't even believe she was doing this. I never thought of doing this growing up; I would be way too scared to leave my parents' house, knowing the trouble I would be in if my parents caught me.

But Laura didn't think that way. She had no fear of us or what was out there and waiting for her. I never could understand that about her, but then again, these were different times, and a lot of kids were acting out, even to the police. They didn't respect anyone, and certainly not the law. That really frightened me. I feared that so much for Laura, knowing the trouble she could get herself into.

When we did catch her sneaking out, we took away her phone or found other ways to punish her. We wanted her to know there had to be consequences for these types of doings and actions. We tried to make her take responsibility for what she did, letting her know that this type of behavior was not okay. No matter how we tried to explain to her that we were concerned for her wellbeing and safety, and that we didn't want anything to happen to her because of how we loved her, it didn't matter to Laura; it's as if she didn't care about us or our feelings and our concerns. It was just so unimaginable to see this and deal with her. I just never thought I would see this beautiful, perfect little girl grow up to do these things and act out this way. I begged her to tell me what I could do to have her stop and open up to me about what was going on in her head or her life to think of doing these things, but she just wouldn't open up; she always looked at us as if 'what she was doing wasn't a big deal and she had it all under control. She wanted us to trust her, but how could we when she just did what she wanted to do and didn't follow the basic rules we gave he or life's rules to having a normal, safe, and healthy life? We struggled over and over as parents in what we could and should do to help our daughter, Laura. I just didn't know anymore when and where this was going to end or get better. I found myself seeking professional help and looking always to God for help and guidance.

I never felt stress like this or the constant worrying. I would feel so hopeless so many times because I was her father looking to fix everything for both me and Laura. I hated the fact that I couldn't fix her or myself. It was so hard for me to accept that I was powerless over all this. Just like in the 12-step program for AA and Nar-Anon, it states for step one, "We admitted we were powerless over alcohol/addict that our lives had become unmanageable." This is what I was experiencing and going through, and it was such a horrible feeling to know 'I couldn't fix this or change Laura and make her be who I wanted her to be. I had to teach myself how to live with it all and live one day at a time, just as an addict does, doing my best each day and moving on to the next. Believing in God, I had to have hope and keep the faith —which was all fine and easy in a perfect world, but not easy for me, who always saw the negative in most things. I had my work cut out for me, as they say; it wasn't going to be easy. But this wasn't about me. It was about Laura and getting her the help she needed and deserved.

As the months passed, our lives just got more complicated and more stressful. Laura was now dating and having boy-friends...or, let's say guys who were her friends. And she liked that, as I said earlier. She loved the attention boys would give her or what they would say to her. For Laura, it was what she wanted and needed. It just gave her such a natural high or lift. Girlfriends couldn't do that for her or give her that feeling. She wanted to be loved and cherished; she wanted what most girls dream of when they are older, not a girl who is only 15. There was no stopping her or turning off these feeling inside of her. She had her agenda already, and it wasn't school or making something of herself. I would constantly remind her she could be anything she wanted in life, and she didn't need boys to help her get there—or need them at all. I told her she had it all, as I had said many times before to her. But again, she couldn't see any of this. Her vision was so blocked and narrow-minded, it's as if she had an addiction to both boys and being out. Laura could just never focused and stay in the moment. She loved to be doing or going somewhere, never being satisfied with where she was at. I saw this as she was growing up, and it never got better, just worse and worse. She would always look to be out with her friends rather than spending time at home with me or her mom. Family was important, but not enough to be satisfied or happy. Happiness for Laura was being out or having a boyfriend. As her father, I never wanted her to have a boyfriend; I knew it would happen, and I couldn't stop it, but I just didn't trust any boy with my daughter. And yes, I knew what was going on, especially in today's times. It wasn't like it was when I was out there dating or going out. It was so out of control and very dangerous, especially being a young, beautiful girl like Laura, who was very naïve and lacked self-esteem.

I also found out as well as her mom did that Laura was using alcohol and smoking cigarettes. Once again, this just showed us she was not changing for the better; just getting worse, which made us more anxious and more worried, if that was even possible at this time. We both were being tested and pushed beyond any parents' limits.

I hated facing and knowing these things about my daughter; I just didn't want to deal with any of it. I prayed and prayed that God would give me the strength or show me what to do. I knew every day would be a challenge and never knew what could happen next. Co-parenting Laura with my ex, we tried to keep each other on the same page and update each other as much as possible or when need be. We had to really work together if we were going to help her as well as help each other.

As the weeks and months went by, we saw our daughter falling deeper and deeper into her addiction of alcohol; a pattern that I saw when I was married to her mom. Lies and manipulation were even becoming stronger, and an everyday occurrence. I would find empty vodka bottles under her bed or hidden in her closet amongst her clothes, and when I would confront her on the empty bottles, she would always have a story or lie, saying they were not hers but her friends, or she was keeping it for a friend. Unlike her mom, who drank beer, Laura was drinking hard liquor. This was really bad and scared me even more. She was aware of her mom's addiction, and her mom had spoken to her about her problems and her addiction, but Laura would always tell us she wasn't going to have a problem with it and she knew what she was doing. I can't tell you how many times I heard that from her. It was as if that was her only answer for all of her wrong doings.

Laura was in total denial. We had kept her therapist in the mix of all her doings and hoped that she could find out what was fueling Laura to want to drink and smoke. Her therapist would tell us that Laura was going to experience change and most likely try alcohol and possibly even mairjuana. This didn't really surprise me because I knew there would be that 50 percent chance that she would suffer with addictions, just as her mom did. It's just the reality of it: When there is one parent who suffers with addiction, the chances of having a child have that addiction is 50 percent, and if both parents have addiction issues, then that chance is even greater with that child or all your children. I didn't want to hear this, but I knew there was nothing I could do about it at, both now and in the future.

It is well known that addiction is a progressive disease, what that means is that the amount of alcohol and drug use increase, as well as the behavioral problems. It is not a disease that stays idol or decreases with time. It's usually a disease that worsens and doesn't get any better.

I just kept wishing that Laura would be more like me and have more of my genes. I knew if that was so, then she could overcome anything. She wouldn't have to worry about not being able to stop or quit a bad habit or addiction. I never had to worry about addictions or bad habits growing up; if I didn't like something I was doing, I could and would just stop. And it's not like I didn't try things in my life as I was growing up. I was very lucky, to say the least. My biggest problem still today is the love of pizza and eating too much of it. Sure, I had the issues of being depressed, and it still overcomes me at times, but by no means does it stop me or slow me down from doing what I want or what I need to do in life or with my life. As we all know, we are all a product of our parents; whether it's good or bad, we are. And there is nothing we can do about that except to be aware of it and accept it. It doesn't mean we have to live with it or have it in our daily lives; we can break the dysfunction and lead a normal and happy life if we choose.

Laura, as we expected, was also smoking pot along with her alcohol usage. She was even smoking it in her bedroom with the window open late at night. So yet again, her behavior and actions were just running wild, and she had no regards for herself or her parents. The self-medicating was always ruling her life and making these bad choices for her. We knew that she didn't want to continue with more self-destruction and have a greater substance abuse along with behavior issues, but this was something she was dealing with every day that passed. Therapists say that we are in control of our body's and ourselves; no one can control us; even though they may try each day, the final decision is ours. Well, this is true for the most part, but with addictions, the addiction—or the Devil, as some will say—is in control and not our minds or brain. I saw that each day with Laura. No matter how she would plan or try to control her daily life for the good, the addiction always won out. Sure, there were the days where we saw positivity in her and her actions, but when we looked further into her day or night, it was filled with lies or manipulation of others or us, all for the better goal of getting what she needed or just plain out using and feeling normal once again.

As Laura now entered high school as a freshman, she got arrested one day while at school. It seems she was carrying a knife in her pocketbook for protection because of cyber bullying from other girls on social media. We were called to the police station to come and pick her up. It was later acknowledged that one of her close friends had turned her in to the principal fearing she would hurt someone with the knife she was carrying. So not only was she arrested, but she was also suspended from school for three days.

After meeting with the principal, we explained how Laura was being bullied and harassed on several different social media sites and mostly all by girls. She was very understanding and assured as that it would be investigated and looked into, but the suspension still stood because of the knife in her possession. As far as the police and the arrest, Laura was a minor, so her record was not that of an adult, and with time, it could be expunged, and no one would ever see it or know about it. Although, we were told that a judge would have view of the file with her arrest as a minor regardless of her current age , so it's never, ever really gone; only there to show your history whether you continue with any more crimes or not. Of course, as her parents, we were really upset about the whole incident and her being arrested at school and placed in handcuffs in front of everyone. I kept thinking, *How will she ever go back to school or face her peers now? But on the other hand, she will probably be known as a tough girl, and people will know: "Do not mess with me ."* This was not something I was proud of, nor did I want anyone to think of her that way. We didn't end up punishing her for the taking of the knife to school but assured her that this kind of behavior is unacceptable and violence is never the answer, nor would we tolerate that as long as she was living with one of us. We did understand how she was scared but never understood taking a knife to school. Myself and her therapist believed she was setting up the cool but tough girl persona or profile. This way, she would be feared by girls but liked by boys. Plus, the town that we lived in was mostly all white-collar and well-to-do families, Laura was well on her way to making a name for herself, and not in a good way. This now just added to the list of problems she already had and raised my stress and worrying even more and more.

Yet again and again, I and her mom were becoming more and more fearful of Laura's future and wellbeing. We knew times were different than when we went to school, and kids were different as well. We expressed ourselves through verbal speaking, not through social media like today. Bullying was done in person, not through Facebook or other social media sites as it is done today.

Laura was really trying to find herself and where she could all fit in her daily life as a teenager. We knew this would be difficult for her but also knew we couldn't do it for her. She was going to have to do it all by herself, but we made sure to tell her that we would always be there for her and that she was not alone in all this.

As the days followed, Laura was very fearful of dealing with school and with the kids who went there. She wasn't like them, and she felt they were definitely not like her. They were all about themselves and in their own world or clique—a place where she was not welcomed or did not belong. Most of the kids in her school came from a good home, and their parents were married, not divorced; stable families with really good incomes. Laura was not comfortable with those types of kids and really didn't want anything to do with them. She just felt her fit was with kids from her old neighborhood and the schools there. Mostly all of her friends were from there, and that's where she would always want to be or hang out. Laura loved being accepted by her own kind; it was a great comfort for her. She could finally be herself, unlike when she was in her hometown and her school there. She related so well to her friends and they to her. Most of them were from broken homes and divorced parents, so she felt truly good about this because she could be herself and not have to act phony or like someone she really wasn't. Most of her friends were all competing, like her, over who was cool and who dared to be bad. They too liked to have fun and were dealing with the Devil himself and his temptations of addiction. School was not a priority to them and certainly not to Laura.

We had to constantly encourage Laura to stick with school and to give her best , not to drop out, and to try to find an interest that she liked while she was there. It made us extremely nervous when she would talk about dropping out. I knew I would have to stay on her to keep her motivated to do whatever it took to keep her mind on not giving up on school and that she had it in her to succeed and graduate.

As her parents, we had to prioritize all of her issues and problems, knowing that we could not help her with all of them and that God had her, as well as us, in this.

As more weeks passed, Laura was interested in getting a job and was looking forward to earning her own money and gaining some responsibility by working. She had just turned

16, and she applied at a pizza restaurant that we would go to not far from our house. The owner, after interviewing her, hired her, and was pleased to have her join his establishment. She too was thrilled, knowing that she got the job right there then and now. She was going to be a hostess, and she was pleased with that since she had a great smile and knew how to greet customers. Plus, she would now earn her own money and not have to ask her parents for everything she wanted to buy. She hated the fact that she always had to ask us when she need something. She wanted to make her own choices when it came to spending money. I totally understood where she was coming from in feeling that way, but I also knew she didn't want us to know that there were going to be the times when the money would be used for drugs, alcohol, or cigarettes. And, of course, there were all the lies that would go with that and her not being honest with us about her real spending.

Laura really liked working and was doing well at her job. She didn't like it when it was slow and she didn't have anything to do there. She said the hours never passed when it was slow with no customers coming into the restaurant. She loved keeping busy, plus I think it controlled her anxiety by working and being busy. She would even help out the waiters and waitresses rather than standing around doing nothing. I told her that made her look really good to the owner and the others who worked there. It showed that she wasn't afraid of working hard and helping out others who could really use her help. This was definitely a good thing for Laura working, and I really think she knew that also. I was very happy for her and was proud that she was taking a step forward with her life and trying good things instead of letting addictions dictate her life and future. She was even thinking about becoming a waitress and trying that. She told me that she could really make good money doing it. I encouraged her to try different jobs because, after all, she was still young, and doing the job was the only way to experience it if she would even like it. I told her all about when I was young and all the jobs I had before I really knew what I wanted to do as far as working and a career. I really wanted to tell her that college was the only way to have a future, but I knew that would be too much for her, and besides, I knew she really wouldn't want to hear it—especially not from me or her mother. I was hoping, somehow, she would see that after working different jobs and seeing there wasn't much money to be made in these jobs; plus all the hard work you would have to put into them to make a decent salary. Here again, I wanted that to come from her and not her dad or her mom trying to convince her we were right for her to just do it. I learned to plant seeds in my daughter's life and that hopefully one day she would remember what I had told her or what we had talked about rather than forcing her to do it. I knew that would never work; it never worked for me or anyone else I knew, so why would it work for Laura?

It was now several months now that Laura was working, and it seemed that she still liked it, which was really good and yet surprising to say the least. She was even working during the week, which I wasn't too happy about because of school and her having such a problem with getting up in the morning and wanting to go to school. She still was drinking and smoking pot. And, of course, this just added to the issue of not wanting to go to school, let alone being tired from working the night before. She was also dating and had a boyfriend who was not a good influence on her and was several years older than her and out of school already. I was not happy about this and knew that nothing good could come of this. Sorry to say; I wasn't trying to be negative, but I knew my daughter and I knew boys, and it seemed Laura liked the bad boys. Why would or should I be surprised in that? After all, nothing was easy when it came to Laura and her life. I knew I had to have hope and try to be positive that this was just a phase and it wouldn't last and she would outgrow this "I like bad boys, and that's who I want to be with" phase. I would constantly tell Laura that I wanted the best for her and for her to have someone who would cherish her and treat her like the queen she was. I made it known to her she deserved the best in every boy who like her or who she liked. I told her to never just settle for any boy or man in life; to be choosey and go for the best. I just wanted her to be loved, just as I and her mom loved her. I knew if she could find someone who would love her unconditionally, even with her addiction, then she would be fine in life, which is something every dad worries about, especially when you have an only child and that child is a girl. It would be different if she had another sibling, especially a brother, then I would know she would be guarded and protected once I was deceased. Just as my dad, who always watched and worried about his two daughters, I too would be faced with this as well. Plus, this wasn't like it was many years ago when my two sisters were dating; this was now so much different and so advanced when it came to boys and men and what they may do to a girl. I was well aware of all this since I didn't live under a rock but knew all that was going on in the current world of dating, or like my daughter would say: "just hanging out." Times were so different compared to when I was young and dating, so much more advanced. I could always hear her say that she could take care of herself and not to worry about her, and that's all fine and good to hear, but in reality, that's not how simple it is, especially for someone like Laura, who didn't always make the best choices.

After several weeks, I was finally able to meet her boyfriend, and this was not easy by any means. She would make every excuse every time I would ask her to meet him. It's as if she didn't want me to meet him. No surprise there. Of course, she didn't want me to meet him because she knew I would not like him or approve of him. She wanted to keep him a secret and not have me know of him or what they were up to. That's who Laura was and how her personality was: to keep everything from her parents. We knew this already after all that we were going through with her in the previous years and dealing with her addiction and behavioral issues.

So here again, we knew we would be faced with lies and manipulation. In therapy, you'll always hear the therapist say, "Just expect it." So very true. This way, it's never a surprise. Great words to live by, especially under these conditions.

Now that I knew who her boyfriend was, it didn't make me feel any better, but only caused me to distrust her and especially him. I wasn't moved by him nor would I ever trust him. He was older and had his own car and didn't seem like he was very responsible all the way around. He was out of school and not really working any full-time job and did not have much of a future or any future plans; at least none that I knew about or any Laura told me about. I knew I wasn't supposed to judge, but we were talking about my daughter here. She was all that I had, and I just didn't trust any boy or man who would be with her or dated her. Her mom and I would discuss how Laura was so trusting of boys only because she wanted them in her life, and when you have addictions and your mind is clouded by all that, you have to be even more careful of who you are with.

Laura was now even having her boyfriend pick her up after work even though I always said I would pick her up all she had to do was call me and I would be there. She was doing this so she could see him and not have to come straight home from work. She would always tell me or her mom that she wouldn't be out long. Here again we were being pushed and tested to our limits and had to deal with more and more each day of what Laura may be throwing at us. I had to keep reminding her it was a school night and that she really needed to be home and not staying out late. Not that she cared; but I cared, and I found myself caring and worrying enough for the whole world when it came to Laura. When I would express this to her, she would either get angry or laugh at me for being that way. She just never seemed to see things as I or her mom did. She was defiantly carefree and lived in her own world, not seeing things as her parents or any responsible adults would see it.

I would constantly bring all these issues to her therapist and would usually call her or email my concerns before Laura would see her for her appointment, but there was only so much her therapist could do or try in order for Laura to see where we were as her parents in raising her and our concerns about her wellbeing all the time. I remember trying anything and everything to help Laura and to make a difference for her life and her future. And if that meant for me to tell or inform her therapist or call her teachers and let them know of her doings and non-doings, then so be it. I would never give up on my daughter, and I reminded Laura of this all the time and would continue to remind her forever if that's what it took to save her.

As the weeks went by, there wasn't much change for the good; instead, there was a decline in both Laura and her actions. She was still staying out and just always had that desire to be out, not finding home to be comforting. It didn't really matter if it was my home or her mom's; she didn't want to be there spending time with her family. And if she was spending time with us, it was short lived, as she was always texting her friends or her boyfriend. Staying in that monument was so very difficult for Laura.

One Saturday night, she came home really high, and she smelled of marijuana. She looked to be also drunk. I didn't know what to do because she was not really responding to me or my voice. I decided to call the police and get help for her as well as for me. The police came out and tried to make sense of it all; they even searched her handbag and found marijuana as well as drug paraphernalia. She ended up being arrested and taken to the police station for processing even though she was a minor. I was so upset, and I called her mom to let her know what took place that evening. Her mom really couldn't handle Laura anymore and was dealing with so many of her own problems and issues. I had Laura living with me now for the time being, knowing that her mom couldn't have Laura anymore. She thought I, too, shouldn't have to put up with Laura and her doings along with her addiction, but I couldn't just shut the door on my daughter, nor would I.

Laura was released later that night and was scheduled for a court hearing in the weeks to come. I knew there was nothing I could do but to have her face the consequences and take responsibility for her doings and actions that night.

I reached out to her school and notified them of what happened. The principal was very understanding and was willing to help her in any way, as well as me. She suggested getting Laura into a drug and alcohol rehab before things got worse. I totally agreed with her on this even though I hadn't reached out to her therapist, yet who I'm sure would have agreed with this suggestion as well. I knew it would also help her with her court troubles if she was in a rehab for her addictions, so I started looking into some addiction rehab facilities in our state of New Jersey. I felt it would be better to stay in the state rather than looking outside of the state. Plus, I knew Laura might be scared and not want to go if it was too far and especially out of state.

After talking to Laura's therapist, she suggested sending her to Princeton House located in New Jersey, which was close to where we were all living. I researched it online and found it to be a rehab center that dealt with both addiction and mental health issues. The reviews were very good, and it seemed like they had helped many who wrote about their stay there, so I set up a phone interview with Laura and gave them all the needed insurance information. After Laura did her phone interview with them, they set up our time to have Laura admitted. I took Laura there the very next day and got her admitted and setup into their program. She was very reluctant at first to go but then realized this was needed for both her and me. She couldn't get better on her own, and she couldn't continue with her current lifestyle and bad choices. I knew I had to make her see that she needed this and the help that they could provide her in getting healthy again and getting her life back.

After saying my goodbyes to her, I assured her that I would be checking up on her and that I would see her soon. Once they allowed me to see her, I would be back, I told her. I was just hoping that she would get as many weeks as needed, but I knew this would come down to the rehab and my insurance regarding her length of stay.

I ended up calling the facility the next day to check on her. I was worried she would be having problems or issues with being there, but I was told and assured she was doing fine. This was a big relief since this was major for me as well as her being away, even though it wasn't far from our home.

After a week, her therapists called me, and we spoke about how Laura was doing and on the progress she was making. Her therapist felt that Laura was very closed and didn't open up much or want to talk about how she felt or what she was feeling inside. I wasn't surprised by this; Laura had always been that way, and it was very hard to get inside of her or find out what she was really feeling. She told me that they would continue to work with her and that hopefully, with more time, she would start to open up. Besides that, she was doing well in group therapy and communicating well with the others she was living with. Not to say that she was speaking much in group, but that was to be expected for Laura. Her therapist also told me I could set up a time to see her on the weekend since that her blackout time was now over. This usually lasts about two weeks at most rehab and treatment centers.

So, the next weekend, I went and saw Laura. I didn't tell her I was coming; I wanted to surprise her. I checked in at the front lobby with the attending aide there and did my sign-in as needed to see her. I then went to the area that was for visitors seeing their loved ones and waited for Laura to arrive from where she was living and staying. Laura finally entered the visiting room from behind a closed door. I was so glad to see her, and yet I was nervous about what to say and how to act. I hugged her and kissed her as if she was gone for a month. She was pleased to see me and seemed to be calm and in control, which I wasn't expecting to see.

We sat and talked all about her stay and how she was doing and feeling. I didn't have a lot of questions for her; I just wanted to keep it cool and collected. I didn't want to make her feel uncomfortable or draw any attention to why she was there and if she liked it. I was pretty much afraid, as always, that she would want out and would be asking for me to take her home, so we just spoke about how proud I was of her, how I knew she could do this, and that things would be great for her once she was done with her stay there. All positive things; and of course, I was building her up for the success she would have after she came home.

Before I left, I told her that I loved her, that I would see her soon, and that there was nothing for her to worry about. Everything would work out. I didn't want to say exactly when I would see her again; I wanted her to stay as long as she needed or as long as the insurance would cover her stay.

The following week, her therapist reached out to me and informed me that she would be released after her 21 days were met. The insurance would only cover her for three weeks, even though Princeton House tried submitting a justification that longer time was needed. I really wasn't thrilled to hear this, but I knew there was nothing that could be done at this point. It's always the insurance that decides what the length time will be, not the rehab—or me, for that matter. I scheduled Laura's pick up that weekend and would also have a sit down with her therapist before she would come home.

I and my wife arrived at Princeton House that Saturday morning hoping that we could meet with her therapist first before Laura's release. I had many questions, and I didn't want to have Laura waiting or feel the pressure of Laura wanting to leave as soon as possible once they brought her out to me. As we checked in at the desk and told them why we were there, they called her therapist as I was standing there. She agreed to come out to see us right away, which was great by my standards. When she came and greeted us, she took us back to her office to talk about Laura's discharge. She filled me in on Laura's progress and her thoughts on Laura and her recovery. She did mention to me again, as before, that Laura was not easy to read nor did she open up much on her feelings. She wanted Laura to continue to work with her therapist and see a psychiatrist to help with her anxiety. I told her I would see to that and thanked her for all her help in treating and working with Laura.

After Laura's three week stay at Princeton House, I tired getting Laura back into going to school. I needed her to try again to attend school and blend in as if she never really left. I wanted her to work on herself and for her to follow what she had learned at Princeton House and all that they had showed her as well as educated her on; who she was and what she could achieve, if she put her mind to it. She agreed to going back and giving it her best. As I always told her, that's all I could ever ask of her: giving it her best.

After several weeks, Laura was doing well again in adapting to school and working with her therapist. I took her also to see a psychiatrist, so she could also be under their care as well.

I wanted Laura to focus on herself and try to limit her friends and going out, for I knew that could lead to trouble or change her thoughts of staying clean. I knew I was asking a lot of her, but I was determined to help her get better and stay that way. I had to make her see all that would be gained from what she learned at Princeton House if she continued using it in her world and in her life.

The next two months were challenging to say the least. It seemed that Laura was struggling in many ways. School was becoming hard again for her, as was going each day. Friends were now becoming a priority, and she was gradually going out more. I spoke to her about all of this and expressed my concerns and feelings towards where this could lead. She, as in the past, said, "I know, Dad. It will be fine."

But I didn't think it would be fine because I just knew it was too tempting to be out with her friends and be exsposed to all their doings and goings. Not good.

As time passed, things just got bad, and Laura started to revert back to where she was not going to school, staying out with her friends, and using again. I had now lost hope on Laura fighting her way back from this hole she had dug for herself. I just couldn't continue to watch her lose everything she worked on at Princeton House. I had to do something besides telling her to leave or figure out her own life and what she wanted it to look like. Sure, I could do that, but Laura wouldn't be able to make that happen even though she would tell you she would and could. I had to help her and would help her regardless.

The next week, I called her principal as well as her therapist and told them about everything that was happening with Laura, specifically how things were getting bad again. They, too, saw it and were concerned as well. Her therapist decided to talk to Laura's principal and decided on some other treatment facilities that would be good for Laura. Her therapist wanted to make sure that her school would work with Laura and grant her the time she needed to get help and seek treatment.

Laura's mom and myself researched treatment centers in New Jersey and found Seabrook Drug and Alcohol Rehab in Bridgeton, New Jersey. It was well-known and highly recommended for substance abusive as well as behavioral problems, and it was only an hour and a half away from our home.

I made the phone call and gave them all the information

needed as well as Laura's contact number, so they could talk to her as well and explain everything about the facility and what she could expect once she was admitted. Laura did agree to go, which was very surprising to say the least. She spoke to her therapist and to the principal of her school about going, and they both were very convincing about her going and getting the help she needed. Her mom talked to Laura and gave her advice and told her about the time she had gone to rehab for her addiction of alcohol. I was glad of that, so Laura could see that her own mom had dealt with this, and it turned out to be positive and changed her whole life as well as saved her life. I wanted Laura to feel totally normal about all this, if that was even possible. I didn't want her to feel like a failure and like this was where her life would end now or this was the end of a normal life. I told Laura how proud I was that she was doing this, that she could do this, and that there was nothing she couldn't accomplish if she put her mind to it. She had this, I kept telling her, and I would tell her not to worry about anything, for I would be there for her no matter what happened, good or bad.

My wife and I ended up taking her the next day to the rehab facility in south Jersey. I was familiar with the area and where it was because I had been down that way before. I knew it was in a rural area, which was good, and not close to anything, which was also a good thing. It's best that way, so you're not distracted by the surrounding area—especially if there is a city or town next to where you are staying. You don't want to have easy access to drugs and alcohol, and that's why the more rural the area, the better.

We dropped Laura off at the front lobby and were not able to stay long, as those are the rules of all rehab and detox facilities when you drop your loved one off. This way, there isn't much time for interaction or for your loved one to change their mind; and I was well aware of this happening and was praying that Laura wouldn't do that. I've watched this on television many times the show *Intervention* on A&E, where that's exactly what would happen; or the addict would end up leaving after the first day. All this was running through my mind, and of course, I was fearing the worst, as always. But thank God, she didn't. So I hugged her and told her I love her and would talk to her soon, even though I knew there is a black out time of usually two weeks, and in that time, no one can call to talk to their loved one. I had known all this already before with Laura's mom when I had dropped her off at rehab before Laura was born. I wasn't sure if Laura remembered from the pre-admission interview she had on the phone about the what the facility required of her. I was concerned as I left her that she might have an anxiety attack where she needed to get out of there or call me or her mom, but I had to keep telling myself that, *I'm sure this happens all the time with other patients...*

I had to convince myself that everything would be okay and not to worry. I kept telling myself that God had this, and He had her. I wanted to believe this so bad, just as all the 12-step programs tells us. Just as the Bible tells us. But knowing me and the way I would always worry about everything, especially Laura, that was easier said than done thanks to my thinking process.

We finally arrived home that evening, and it was a quiet ride home; such a sad ride home for me. I just had dropped off my little girl, my everything, at this faraway and strange place that I really knew nothing of, except what they told me and what I read about it. I had to hold on to hope and pray that this was the right thing to do and that she would get the help she needed and deserved. That's all I had at this point, and I had to believe that this would make her better and save her life, so she could have a future. It was so hard to know that she was all alone in a strange place with strange new people again; people who were like her and suffering with their own problems and their own addiction. I just wanted her home where she belonged, not at a rehab. But I had to come to terms and faced reality. I had to accept that she couldn't be home until she was well, and no matter what I wanted for her, I couldn't get her until she got the help she needed.

I didn't sleep much that night, although you would think I would because she was under lock-and-key, safe from both the world and herself. I did go to work that day, but it was not very productive since my mind was racing from wondering how she was doing and handling everything in rehab. I knew they would have her on a schedule and that she would be busy all day with meetings, both group and one-on-one, along with a whole list of requirements and other activities related to her.

As I said earlier, it was a waiting game of two weeks before I could talk to her or find out how she was doing. I was hoping they would reach out to me before the two weeks to give me an update, otherwise I was going to reach out to them. There was no way I was going to wait to hear about how my daughter was coping and doing. My anxiety level was elevating each day that went by without me knowing what was going on where she was, wondering about her wellbeing. And yes, you would think I would be okay because she was just at Princeton House not that long ago.

Finally, a week had gone by, and her counselor called me with an update. I was so glad that he did and couldn't wait to hear about how she was doing and if she was coping and getting along with everyone as well as the facility itself. Her counselor, who was a man, which I thought that was very surprising, was very knowledgeable and very understanding of me wanting to hear everything, along with my million questions that I had for him. We ended up speaking for close to an hour on the phone, which was very pleasing to me. He was very happy with Laura and how she was doing so well even though it was only a week. He informed me that the first week is the toughest for all newcomers and that most will end up leaving in the first day or 24 hours, so I was really glad to hear that she survived a week already and that she wasn't fighting it or causing problems for everyone there. I knew how Laura could be and how she could be very manipulative and forceful in getting her way or what she needs. After all, this is how most addicts cope for the most part. They have no problem when it comes to using people or lying, stealing, or cheating to get their way or what they need from you. It's classic behavior, and Laura was very good at all of this. She also could be as sweet as can be and fool everyone, then turn when she didn't get her own way. This was a behavior that she learned early in her childhood years and perfected as she got older, so I was always expecting it because she used it on me and her mom so many times. Why should rehab be any different?

In the weeks to follow as Laura was there, I learned that my insurance would only cover her for a total of 30 days at rehab, and there was also a good chance they would cut her off after 21 days, so now I had this to worry about, especially since she was doing so well there. The last thing I wanted was her to be cut off early from getting the help she needed.

In the end, Laura was only able to stay a total of 28 days. I had tried to get her more time both by reaching out to my insurance and the rehab itself, but that didn't work, and that's all my insurance was going to be paying for. They, the insurance and the rehab facility, did tell me that I could pay out of pocket if I wanted her to stay longer, and it would cost me a $1,000 a day. I wish I had that kind of money, for I would have gladly have paid for my daughter to stay another month or more if needed. I just knew that wasn't possible, even though I knew the more time she stayed in treatment, the better her chances were that she wouldn't use again once she came home or was released. All the studies and readings dealing with addiction show that most addicts need a 90-day treatment plan in order for them to have the greatest success rate possible.

So, after 28 days of treatment, Laura was being released. I went to pick her up and meet with her counselor to discuss the progress she had made while being in treatment and her recommended discharge care. I first met with her counselor, where we spoke about Laura and her treatment plan while she was there for the 28 days. He spoke highly about her and was very pleased with the work she did during her time there, working with him and her therapist, and in her group meetings. He felt she really accomplished a lot and wanted to get better, and as we all know, it's about wanting it. We can want it for our loved one, but if they don't want to get better and change their ways, then it will never work; and he felt she wanted the change in her life and not to continue to be an addict. I, of course, was very pleased to hear this and was hoping this was the truth and that Laura wasn't just saying that to please those she was working with. I know how Laura could be, and she was very good at it when it came to telling people what they wanted to hear. Again, this is typical addict behavior, not something Laura was doing that no one else has ever done before.

After we spoke for quite some time about Laura and her care, he went and got Laura, so I could finally see her. When she came out, I was so thrilled and happy to see her; it seemed like it was forever since last saw her. I hugged her tight and told her how much I missed her. She looked different, and not in a bad way. Just different. Her color was off since they didn't really go outside much, so maybe she was lacking vitamin D. She seemed calm and relaxed and in control; something that I hadn't seen her do or show in a long time. I was happy to see that in her. It made me feel like she had changed in a positive way.

We all sat down and talked about her care in coming home and what she needed to do or should do to stay clean and sober. Her counselor told her that she had what it took to succeed with her addiction and her behavioral issues. He felt confident that she could do this and that he would be checking up on her in the days and weeks to follow. He told her that she was not alone in all this and that help was always there, especially if she did her meetings every day.

Meetings are really important in any addiction and a 12-step program. Meetings are known as your lifeline, and it's important to get a list of people who will always be there for you, that you can call at any time. I told her that I would take her to her meetings and even go and sit with her in them. I didn't want her to feel scared or alone. I told her I would support her in any way I could.

I wanted her to know I wasn't just saying this because of her counselor sitting there. I wanted her to know she could always count on me, regardless. Her counselor told her that she was very lucky to have a dad who was there for her and would help her in any way he could. He said that is important to have family behind you and to have their support. Many addicts don't have that family support—or any help for that matter, which makes it that much harder to stay clean and to have any future. I really thought Seabrook was much more intense and more thorough with greater structure for the addict than Princeton House.

We gathered up all of her belongings and headed home. Laura was glad to see Helen as well. I felt bad for Laura knowing she would have liked her mom to be there, but I knew that wasn't going to happen because of her anxiety issues, and traveling in a car that far was difficult for her.

When we got home, we got Laura settled in to her room, and I tried to make her comfortable in any way I could. I knew this was going to be hard for her after being locked in for 28 days at rehab. I was afraid for her because I knew she had trouble sleeping, and that's where the alcohol and drugs came into play in order for her to relax and sleep. They had suggested for her to try reading before bedtime or taking melatonin. I had given her that before, but she would always say it didn't work for her. I knew that was the issue because of her severe anxiety.

Laura gradually started going to school again but decided to enroll in vo-tech and take up cosmetology. I encouraged her to pursue this if that meant she would stay in school. I felt it was a good thing for her since she wasn't into the academia of school and all that went with it. Plus, she would learn a skill that she would always have to fall back on, even if she did go to college one day. I was desperate to get her to stay in school and at least graduate. Also, her principal was willing to help her out in any way she could, which was a true blessing for both Laura and myself.

Laura was attending meetings for her addiction, and I would take her as much as possible or whenever she needed a ride. She was trying to cope with it all and deal with her friends, a lot of whom were really only friends when she would go out and party with them. She knew she had to pick and choose who her friends were. Otherwise, staying clean and sober was really going to be a problem. I told her it had to be her choice because telling her what she needed to do would not work; plus, the last thing she needed was her father telling her again and again what to do. She needed to stay away from her boyfriend who was a bad influence on her as well as all her other male friends. She had heard this from me a thousand times before.

I have to say she was trying to do the right thing every day; it's just that her mind was telling other things to do. I even saw she had a list of names and numbers of people from her meetings that were there to help, and they were just a phone call away. Here again, this was really important for her to have this list to fall back on, too; this was her support system. They could help her in ways that I couldn't. These were people like her, struggling every day with the same issues and addiction as her. They knew what she was going through and her pain that she had to deal with. Her mom would try to help her also because she, too, was doing her meetings and had over 24 years of being sober. She would also take Laura to meetings and would introduce her to all her female friends in her sobriety circle.

Her mom thought it would be a good idea for Laura to see a psychiatrist as well as a therapist who had experience dealing with those who suffer with addiction, so we found both for her, and she was put on meds for both depression and her anxiety. I would take her to her psychiatrist as well as her therapist, hoping that they could help her deal with all that she had going on in her life. I also had her counselor checking in from Seabrook House to see how she was doing. They, too, wanted the best for her and cared about her wellbeing. I was glad that they were checking in on her. It made her see that many people really cared about her and the problems she was dealing with.

Laura was doing great in vo-tech and seemed to really like it. She was very talented in doing both hair and makeup. This didn't really surprise me because I always felt she was gifted in so many ways. She always picked up fast on everything. She reminded me of myself and how diversified I was and how I was good at so many things. I loved that about myself and was glad Laura had this ability as well. I knew the more she could do, the better off she would be in life. I didn't want her to have to depend on others. I myself hated to have to depend on others, so I tried to teach myself and learn so many different things.

After several months of Laura going to both school and vo-tech, along with keeping up with her AA meetings, I decided to buy her a car. This way, she could drive herself to school in the morning and home after school. I felt this would be a good test to see if she was ready for the responsibility of having a car. I knew this was taking a big chance and was told by others that I should really think about this and what could happen.

She had gotten her driver's permit when she was 16 and had drivers' education in high school. She passed her driver's test the first time and had great driving ability and confidence when she was behind the wheel. I decided to give her Helen's car, which was a small but well-maintained Toyota Corolla. Helen then bought a new car, and I paid her for selling me her Corolla to give to Laura. It was a really nice car; nothing like what I had when me and my twin started to drive. I wanted her to have something safe and reliable; a car that I knew wouldn't break down on her or need a lot of repairs.

She was really happy and thrilled that I bought a car and couldn't wait to drive it. I explained to her it was only to be used for school, and anything else would have to be cleared with me. She was okay with this, so I decided to give this a try and give her a chance on this huge responsibility; not to mention the cost to me of both buying the vehicle and the insurance.

I remember the first day she took it to school and me taking pictures of her and her car; it was like taking pictures of her on her first day of kindergarten. Both me and Helen thought she looked so cute driving it. It was a perfect fit for her; not too big of a car but the right size and manageable.

Things seemed to be going well the first couple of weeks as she drove it to and from school. She then started to ask me if she could drive it to her boyfriend's house after school. I was a little bit hesitant about this even though I knew where he lived and met him several times already. I kind of knew that this wasn't going to be easy, and if you gave Laura an inch, she would ask for more and more, so I had to be ready and have my guard up at all times because she was going to test me as she would always do. I told her that I didn't want her to stay out late with the car, and if she wasn't going to come home before it got dark, I would go and get the car. I didn't want her to drive in the dark; not yet at least.

So as the weeks went by, Laura was driving to her boyfriend's house and staying late, as I thought she would do. I put up with it in the beginning and went several times to pick up the car and drive it home. She then was allowed to drive it at nighttime, but that also was pushing it and my patience was tested as well. I told her I didn't want her to stay out late with the car and that I would come and pick up the car if I knew she was going to be out late. So sure enough, that's what was and kept happening. Finally, I took the car away from her until she could do what I wanted her to do. She would tell me over and over that she could meet my needs, but she always resorted back to doing what she wanted to do. I also had a problem with her keeping the car clean, especially on the inside. I didn't feel like I was asking a lot from her regarding her responsibilities in having a car. She was so good at promising me about taking care of the car and following my rules, but she just could never follow through or be consistent with what I expected of her when it came to her car.

As time went by, I decided to give her another chance regarding her car. Once again, things went well in the beginning, and she was doing what she needed to do and what I wanted her to do. But then as the weeks went by, I noticed she was coming home under the influence, which led me to believe that not only was she using but was also driving like this. I even found alcohol in the car in plain sight, not even hidden. I now knew I couldn't have this or allow this to continue. She could kill someone and even injure herself for that matter. One night, she even took the keys when I wasn't looking and took the car.

She just couldn't control herself regarding the car and the use of it. She left me no choice but to sell the car and be done with all of it. I was so upset to say the least. I really tried, and I wanted it to all work out for her. I thought she could have a car like so many young teenagers. I probably wanted it more than she did. But I now knew this was not in God's plans, or hers. I ended up putting the car on Craigslist, and it sold within two weeks to a family who wanted it for their daughter who was attending college. I was happy to see that someone would make good use of it and was hoping everything would work out for them.

I was now back to trying to figure out where we go from here since Laura was using again and back to her old ways. She would tell me that she wasn't really using or drinking much. That was just her way of downplaying that she was getting high or using like in the past. You either use or you don't; there is no such thing as using "a little" or drinking "a little." All addicts use to meet their needs, and their needs are to use as much as needed. They themselves never know how much they may need to get high; they may have a general idea, but it will never be "very little" or to have "just one" drink. Anyone who doesn't have an addiction or is an addict can make that statement," "I'm just going to have one drink" or "I will just do one line of cocaine." An addict can't stop once they start to use; they just can't say no. I was very educated now on substance abuse, and Laura knew this, so every time she tried to sell me the lines: "I can stop anytime I want," "I only drink a little," or "I don't really get high much," I knew this was not her talking but the addiction, and I always knew she would stop at nothing.

I started to look into getting her more help and researching other treatment facilities. I didn't want her to go back to Seabrook House even though I thought highly of the place. I wanted her to try someplace different; someplace that could get her more rehab time. I also knew that Florida treatment centers had a system of where they could get you more than 30 days and have the insurance agree to it. It was set up to where you would live and one facility and then do your treatment at another. This way, they could bill the insurance separately unlike going to one rehab and stay there the entire time. This was the way they got the insurance to give the client/patient more rehab time. I was glad to learn this and was eager to have Laura try it. I wasn't crazy about the idea of her going to Florida, especially by herself, but if it got her the time and treatment she needed, then why not? I would first have to see if she would do it or agree to going to Florida.

Several people I knew who dealt with addicts and their own addiction recommended Behavioral Health of the Palm Beaches (BHOP). They were located in south Florida and had a very good reputation with helping addicts with both their addiction and their mental behavioral issues, so I decided to call them and get all the info needed to make my decision. Here again, it wasn't just up to me but up to Laura wanting to go to get the help she needed.

After speaking to admissions and getting all the information I needed, I then decided to speak to Laura about it and what I knew of the place from my phone call. When I went to speak to Laura about my phone conversation regarding BHOP, she told me that she was looking into drug and alcohol rehabs in Florida. She wanted to go to Florida because she was told by some of her friends and people in the program that Florida would be a good fit for her. So there it was: I was concerned about her being scared of going out of state, especially a state like Florida that is over 1,000 miles away, and here she was deciding and planning on it already. I wasn't sure if she just wanted a change in her life by going to Florida or if she really wanted to help herself and get clean. I decided to sit down with her and talk all about BHOP and about her looking into drug and rehab facilities on her own in Florida. She told me that she really wanted to go to Florida—and all for the right reasons: to get clean and stay sober. She felt going to Florida would be good for her, and that the treatment centers there had a much higher success rate in dealing with addiction and the addict themselves. She was very convincing, that's for sure, and it seemed genuine. I didn't want to say no to her since she wanted to go, and how could I say no if she wanted to get clean and work on her addiction and problems? So I told her make the call and give them all the information they needed to allow her admission into their treatment program.

My insurance always okayed Laura for treatment no matter if it was in state or not. I was very fortunate to have such great coverage that my job provided, otherwise it would be at least a $1,000 a day for treatment. And if she needed to be detoxed, that would be much higher per day, anywhere between $1,000 and $2,500.

BHOP informed me and Laura that they would arrange and pay for her flight. She just needed to tell them when she would be coming. She wanted to leave as soon as possible, and I was okay with that. She was sent all the information needed for the flight, and they would pick her up at the airport once she landed. She was scheduled to leave in less than two days after the arrangements were made with BHOP. I helped her pack everything she would need because they gave us a list, just as Seabrook Rehab House did, of products that were okay to bring. Nothing with alcohol was allowed, and any meds would be checked once she got there. They were very strict, and you had to follow the rules they implemented in order for them to help you on your road to recovery.

I drove her to the airport on the day she was to depart for BHOP. I felt nervous for her, and I knew she was under the influence, which is normal for addicts before they check in for treatment. I was always proud of her for going for treatment since that most addicts turn down treatment even if its free. And even if they don't want to get clean, there is always that chance that once they do enter treatment, they will want it.

It wasn't easy for Laura, even if she told me she was okay with going. That was just her way to say, "I'm scared and don't really want to go." I, too, always found myself doing that, not telling anyone what was really going on inside of me. I took her all the way to Transportation Security Administration (TSA), where she would have her luggage and ID checked. I wanted to take her right to the gate, but that wasn't allowed anymore, so I had to say my goodbyes to her there at the TSA checkpoint. I showed her the act that most parents would show their child when they are leaving: the act of being calm and cool. No worries telling her she could do this and that she had all she needed if she just looked to herself and inside herself. I hugged and kissed her tight and told her that I loved her and that I would visit her as soon as I was allowed. She was happy to hear this. I knew once again that her mom couldn't be there for her, so I had to be both parents for her. I had no problem telling her that I would see her soon because I would travel to the moon for Laura, and I know she knew this. There would be nothing to stop me unless I was deadly sick in going to see her, regardless what state or what country she was or was to be in. I never, ever put conditions on Laura, especially when it came to her addiction and mental behavior. I knew she never wanted any of this, and how could I blame her for her actions or her doings? I just couldn't believe she was on to yet another rehab. I had to remain hopeful and positive for both of us.

I watched her go through TSA and then walk to her gate until she disappeared and was out of my sight. I told her to text me when she was on the plane and when she landed in Florida.

And sure, enough by the time I got to my car at the airport parking lot, she had texted me she was on the plane and just waiting for it to take off. Once again, I was so sad and depressed that my little girl was now on her way to a third rehab for drugs and alcohol. And it was a thousand miles away—too far to just jump in a car and be there in several hours. I had to keep telling myself that this was about Laura and not me and my issues or feelings. I had to convince myself that she was going to get better this time and get her young life back once and for all. I knew she was in good hands and that BHOP had a really good reputation in helping those who couldn't help themselves with addiction.

After about an hour of driving, I was finally home. Now I would wait to hear from Laura that she had landed safely and was being picked up by a representative of BHOP. Sure enough, after close to three hours, she texted me that she was picked up and on her way to BHOP. I was so relieved to hear this and now knew she was there and would be taken care of and treated for her addiction and her anxiety. I felt like now maybe I could sleep and maybe not worry so much about her. Even though I would worry about her being away so far, at least I knew she was safe, and nothing could happen to her because she was in a lockdown facility. It's almost like being in prison where you know you can't use or escape; you are watched and accounted for each day; and it's all for your best and wellbeing.

In the following weeks, I was allowed to call and check up on Laura and talk to her therapist as well as her counselor. She just completed her second week at BHOP and was doing well according to her therapist and counselor. I also got to talk to Laura, and she sounded very positive and upbeat, which was definitely a good sign. It was great to her voice after two weeks of blackout time and no phone calls. I really missed her and was glad that the two weeks were over. Just like when she was a Seabrook House, the time seemed like forever before I could speak to her or know how she was doing.

They informed me that she was on different meds for her anxiety and was always being monitored for that. They were meds that were approved by the psychiatrist who was seeing her there. They informed me that they never prescribed meds that were addictive. Any rehab or detox facility will never and should never prescribe meds that could be addictive in the long run.

I was very pleased to hear of her progress and that she was doing so well. I told them I was planning on coming down to drop off some things she needed in the days to follow. I wanted to see for myself where she was living and the area itself. I was told by management that I couldn't see her or where she was living. This was for security reasons. This way, no one could come and take her out or drop off drugs or alcohol. I totally understood their rules and was in agreement with that. The last thing I wanted was to jeopardize Laura's treatment, but parents should always do a personal visit if they can and not just take the rehab staff's words on the progress of their loved one.

We booked our flight that weekend to go see the town where Laura was at; my wife was coming with me as well.

We arrived in Florida that weekend and rented a car to drive to the address that was given to us. She was staying at cottages that were separate from the facility. As I mentioned before, this was the Florida model of how you are able to get more time when you live off site from where your treatment is. She was staying somewhere in Lake Worth, Florida, but we had to go to the offices to drop off what she needed us to bring down to her.

We had no problem finding the address that was given to us to drop off her things. It was a small office building in the town of Rivera Beach, which is not far from Lake Worth. I met a woman there who knew Laura, and I was able to leave her things with her. She told me that they were staying not too far away, and it was located on the water. I remember Laura telling me that also, and that the sunsets were really beautiful at dusk. I really wished I could have seen her, but rules are rules, and again, it was all for the best.

We ended up driving around the area and making an adventure of where we thought she could be staying in Lake Worth. It actually seemed like a nice area and would be good for any person, especially someone dealing with addictions who would crave sunny skies, warm weather, and the beach. These are all good things for those who are struggling with addictions, depression, and other behavioral problems.

We stayed several days in Florida and enjoyed the warm weather, the beautiful beaches, and the different areas of south Florida.

I spoke to Laura days later, and she informed me that she got everything we brought down to her. She told me she was doing well, and she still sounded positive about being there. I was in touch with her therapist and counselors on a week-to-week basis. Everything seemed good so far.

Most addicts seem to struggle the more time they get because they are withdrawing, and this can wear on them. Many of us may think that the more time an addict has, the easier it will be on them and their addiction. That's not necessarily correct. It's the actually the opposite, and this was the case for Laura; they really struggle and want to use. This was my biggest fear and nightmare. This is where you will hear, "Take it one day at a time." And that's exactly why addicts need to do this, so they do not become overwhelmed with each day.

Well, it seemed my biggest fear became a reality on Laura's

30 days of being sober at BHOP. She called me saying she had just left BHOP with a friend and was going to live in a sober living home. I couldn't believe what I was hearing from her. I thought I must be dreaming. I was so upset with her and mad at her for just leaving BHOP without even calling me to discuss this. I knew this couldn't be good; she must have just walked out without even telling anyone there she was thinking of leaving or discussing her unhappiness of the place and their treatment. I had figured out by now, she must have used in order for her to just leave like that. She kept telling me that it was all for the best, and she would be fine. I still was in shock from hearing all this I thought she was happy there and was doing so well and wanted to stay there and work the program. Boy was I really wrong on this one. She then told me she had to go and would call me once she knew where the sober living home was that her friend was going to take her to.

I didn't want to hang up with her; I was so scared for the two of us now. Here she was now on her own in Florida, where supposedly some friend was going to help her find a place to live. This was so crazy, and I just couldn't even process it without shaking inside from my worries and fears.

I called BHOP as soon as I hung up with Laura and spoke to her therapist. She informed me that yes, it was true Laura left. But the real reason was that she had got caught using. Someone had gotten her alcohol to consume, and she was caught with it. I was so let down from hearing all this, and it just really saddened me so much. Here I thought she was doing so well and was making progress each day that went by. But as we all know, addicts can't just turn off a switch for their addictions, and I knew this would be hard for Laura no matter what she really wanted for her life now or for her future.

BHOP did tell me that she could come back, but she would have to be cleared through their detox program first. I didn't know if Laura would be willing to do that since she already made up her mind and was moving into a sober living home. Where, I didn't even know; and how she would even do this? I couldn't even get in touch with her, so this was not going to be easy at all to find out what she was up to or doing. Here again, I was trying to keep it all together and stay calm and positive without really freaking out. Plus, I was just hoping her cell was not broke and was working. I can't tell you how many cell phones I had bought Laura throughout the years—many of them dropped or lost due to her being under the influence.

The next day, I finally heard back from Laura because when I tried to call her, her phone went to voicemail or was off. She found a sober living home to go to that a friend got her into and was already there as we were speaking. I really wasn't too crazy about any of this: her being all alone in this house where she didn't know anyone and she didn't even know the area or where she really was. She wanted to try this and felt that it would work out and be fine. Again, I said to myself, *No, this isn't going to work,* and *What could Laura be thinking?*

By the second day, Laura called me telling me she was really scared to stay there. She was in the house with some older woman who she knew nothing of and didn't feel safe at all with this woman living there with her. Plus, she had no money or anything to eat. It seems her friend who found her this sober living home didn't tell her all the details or the truth. Some friend that was.

After hearing all of this, I told her I wanted her to come home as soon as possible. And she agreed and didn't fight me at all on this. I told her I would make all the arrangements to fly her back home, and I would call her as soon as I had her flight booked and her ride back to the airport.

I got working right away on booking her a flight for the next day; I didn't care what it was going to cost. I needed her to be safe and back home in New Jersey with me.

I was able to get her a flight back home for the next day and also got her a taxi to pick her up at the address she gave me. I was extremely lucky to find a taxi company that accepted credit cards since that Laura had no money to pay for a ride to the airport. I had God working with me, and He was showing me the way because I knew I couldn't do this by myself.

I then called Laura once I had all the flight information and gave her everything she needed, along with the taxi service that would be picking her up the next afternoon. I had to walk her through it all, so she wouldn't miss her flight. It was so difficult to explain everything to Laura since I wasn't there to show her what needed to happen or be done for tomorrow's flight. Even though Laura was extremely smart, she was on her own with no one to help her in a state that she knew nothing of or her whereabouts.

I made sure Laura knew she could call me anytime that day or night if she felt scared or unsafe. Tomorrow couldn't come fast enough for me. I knew I wouldn't be able to sleep until she was on her way back home.

That morning, Laura called me saying she was packed and ready to leave. I was so relieved to hear that. I reaffirmed the time that the taxi was coming to get her and asked for her to call me or text me as soon as she was in the cab and on her way to the airport. An hour after we spoke, she was texting me that the taxi came and got her. I didn't tell her, but I called the taxi service asking them to call me once they arrived at the address that I gave them, so either way, I had it covered. I couldn't afford for her to not get to the airport and/or miss her flight. I knew it was best I didn't tell her this, otherwise she would be mad that I didn't have faith in her and believe that she could do this by herself.

She assured me that she would let me know once she was boarding and would be on the plane. After waiting for what seemed like forever, she finally texted me that she was on the plane and was just waiting to take off. Thank God!

Now I just needed to wait for her to reach out to me and tell me that she had landed, and I would then meet her at the gate. I got to the airport early and was already at the gate where her plane would be coming in. I kept checking the travel board at the terminal telling me that her plane was on time. I couldn't wait to see her. My anxiety level was crazy. I just wanted her back in New Jersey, safe and sound.

After about a half hour she texted, telling me she was coming off the plane, and she would look for me. Within several minutes of talking to her, I could see her, and my worries were finally over. She made it back. I hugged her and kissed her tightly, telling her she was home and safe.

We left the airport once we got to my car and headed home. We really didn't talk about what happened at BHOP. I felt that could be done later. I just wanted her to feel at ease and not to add more to the whole situation of what happened and what she did to cause all of this. Of course, there was my disappointment in her and what had happened down in Florida, but I had to accept this was how it was always going to be having a daughter who has an addiction. Even in recovery, she would always be an addict, and nothing would change that or her behavior and her actions of everyday life. I had to accept this, and as the professionals say, you have to just accept this. This is their normal, unlike those who don't have or suffer with drug and alcohol addiction.

When we got home, we got her unpacked and settled in, just as we did when she came home from Princeton House and Seabrook House. She was happy to be home but feared what lay ahead for her and what would be expected of her once again. I told her we would take it one day at a time, and we would all work together so that she could succeed and not feel alone in all of this.

In the next couple of months, I enrolled Laura into night school for vo-tech, so she could finish her cosmetology degree. I also reached out to her principal at her high school and got the needed assignments in order for her to finish her school-work so she could graduate. She wouldn't be graduating with her class because of all the time that passed and all the days that were missed, but at least she would be graduating. This was a huge relief for both me and her that she could graduate high school and vo-tech. I know I wanted it so bad for her because she wasn't living a normal teenager's life or following any of her dreams. Inside, her addiction was ruling her life and driving her down the wrong path.

It wasn't easy having her living at home and still going out with her friends. I still expected her to follow the rules as always and for her to stay clean no matter what. She knew this wasn't going to be easy all the way around, especially graduating from both high school and vo-tech. But like I kept telling her, she could do it, and I would be there to help anyway I could. And I was. I made sure she always had a ride to vo-tech and meetings, just as I did in the past; nothing had changed, and I made sure she always knew that.

I felt really bad that she couldn't be with her class regarding graduation, but once again, this was out of her hands and must be given to God. I did get her cap and gown, so she could wear it to have photos taken. She didn't want this at all, but my wife Helen got her to take a photo for me in her cap and gown. This meant the world to me, for I knew she was only doing it for me and not herself. Laura, as always, was just ready to move on and be done with it. This is how she felt about high school and the graduation part. I totally understood how she felt because it's exactly how I felt when I graduated. I just wanted out and for it to be over. And yes, I went to my gradation, but that was it. I was so thrilled for it to be over. I looked at it like I was doing time in jail and that it would never end. Laura definitely took after me in that aspect. I could never tell her any of this because she would then say, "See, Dad? And you talk about me"..."

I always had to think twice of what I could tell her or share with her, otherwise it might come back to haunt me.

The day finally came where Laura was finally finished with both high school and vo-tech. She had made it. I was extremely proud of her. She accomplished it all, and it was all behind her now.

In several weeks, she would be getting her high school diploma mailed to her. All she needed to do now was take the state board test for her cosmetology license for state of New Jersey. I knew this would be easy for her because she was so smart and talented as a cosmologist. She wasn't worried at all either. Helen was going to be her model for the test. She just needed to pass the written and practice test.

On the day of her test, Laura stayed out late the night before even though I told her she had her test the next morning and she really shouldn't go out. She was hung over from drinking and was tired as well. But somehow, she was able to pass both with a score of 85. I couldn't believe it; I was shocked to say the least. Here I thought for sure she had failed both of the tests, but instead, she did very well.

It is said and is proven that those with addictions are extremely intelligent. Most might think they are not and can't accomplish anything in life, but that is so not true. So many addicts have degrees and have or have had very important positions and jobs in life. They may have lost everything because of their addiction and nothing else. Laura was always smart and picked up fast on anything you taught her or showed her. Her mom was the same: extremely intelligent and could accomplish anything she put her mind to even though she struggled with her own addiction.

In the weeks to follow, Laura looked for jobs as a cosmetologist and as a waitress as well. She was now 19 years old. She never had a problem finding a job. What she did have was a problem with showing up for the job once she got it. Her anxiety always took over, and now, fear would set in, having her not show up for her first day of work or training. Using would help her cope with all of this in going to work. But once she started using, her attendance for that job would decline until she just stopped going to work and would just quit or not even call them to quit. This was very common for Laura and was just an endless cycle when it came to employment and working.

She was able to get a barber position at Sport's Clips. She really did well there even though she never cut man's hair and picked up fast with the training that they gave her. She was making good tips because men usually tip well and she liked working there. After about a month of working, she was struggling with separating herself from going out and working and going to meetings. Again, her addiction was winning over and controlling her. She finally just ended up quitting this job as well. The vicious cycle of addiction just continued for Laura.

Again, I began looking into getting her treatment because she was not doing well in staying clean. I was able to find a detox center in south Jersey, about an hour from our home. She would need to go there first and then to a rehab that was very close to our home known as Footprints Recovery Treatment Center. I then made all the phone calls needed to get her in.

It would be convenient for her to be so close to home, and this way, if she needed anything, I could be there in no time. She spent five days in detox and then was taken to Footprints Treatment Center. She ended up staying there a total of 30 days before being released to a sober living house (SLH) down towards the shore area. Her mom was able to come with me to take Laura and get her set up in the SLH.

She was doing well there for several weeks and even got a job as a receptionist at a hair salon. I went to visit her at her job, and she really seemed happy, and the people there were very pleased with her as well. The following week, the house manger called me up only to tell me that her and another girl living at the home left to go use and come home under the influence, so she would have to leave because this house only gave everyone one chance and then you were asked to leave or check yourself into a detox program.

I ended up taking Laura home but only to look for another rehab and treatment center that would be able to help her. I once again had no choice because if I took her home, she would just continue to use, and I didn't have the heart to just throw out to the streets even though so many said I should. She was a girl, and she was my daughter; I just couldn't do it or live with that decision.

I found a rehab facility in Lancaster, Pennsylvania, called Retreat Behavioral Health that my insurance covered as well. It had a very good reputation for dual diagnosis and was highly recommended by those I knew. I made all the arrangements on my end for Laura to go, but I now needed her to call and do the phone interview as she had done with all the other previous rehabs. Laura felt she didn't need to go and assured me again she could stay clean. I told her that this wasn't up for discussion, and she needed to go. I reminded her that she could not live with me if she wasn't going to stay clean and live by my rules. Not working, not staying clean, and not going to meetings wasn't working for both her and me. She knew this already. She had been told this so many times before. She was also stealing from me and my wife and had even sold my PlayStation that I had got for Christmas to buy drugs. I also caught her taking my wife's car without even asking her. I could have reported it to the police as stolen, and she would have gone to jail. But I didn't, and I couldn't, do that; I felt that was not the answer even though many said I should have called the police and told them she stole it.

I knew Laura needed help again, and that she was just spinning out of control. This was my life with an addict as a daughter, and even though I knew this with each day that passed, it was still hard to for me to accept it.

Addicts will always lie; it's all part of the addiction and their life. They will steal from everyone and anyone if needed. They cannot be trusted and will fool you and hurt you every time you think they can be trusted. They will take all kinds of chances, even if it means they will get caught and get arrested or do jail time. This is not what they want at all, but they cannot control themselves or the addiction that runs within them. I remember so many people saying to me, "Why don't addicts just stop?" or "Why doesn't your daughter just stop using?" Those who say that don't really understand addiction or what drives addiction. They think it's just a switch or a button you can hit or just turn off anytime. If only it was that easy and controllable... There wouldn't be any addicts then.

It's not an addict's fault; it's the disease they have, and you'll never be able to reason with them as you would with someone else who has no addiction. These are just the facts and nothing more. And by accepting all of this, it will make your understanding of your loved one and their life more tolerable.

We were finally able to have Laura accepted after making all the necessary phone calls and supplying my insurance information to Retreat rehab, so the next day, I drove Laura to Retreat in Lancaster. I took her to the admissions center of the facility, and we then said our goodbyes. It was very sad for me and her, just like all the other times dropping her off at rehabs. I really hated this, and I'm sure she felt the same, but I just didn't know what more I could do at this point or how I could save her. I needed her to be clean and sober, and she needed it as well if she was to have a chance at life—any kind of life for that matter.

Nar-Anon gives you the advice of cutting off the addict or your loved one. They tell you should have their phone turned off if they have one, and you should not enable them in any way. No money; no rides; no nothing. You should even tell them to leave if they are not going to stay clean living under you roof. Now, what you can do for them or tell them is that you will help them in any way to get clean and sober, but that's it. They need to have consequences for their actions and doings, and that's the bottom line. I mean, I really feel this is hard advice, but if you think you can do it, then that's on you and not what Nar-Anon is telling you. Plus, I feel this is just advice or some tips and steps you can take. Nothing here is a sure fix or is guaranteed to work. And also, you will have to live with your choices—especially if you throw them out into the streets and you never see or hear from them again or, God forbid, they die out there.

I remember expressing myself and sharing to others in my Nar-Anon meeting that this life with Laura was hell for me, but it was especially hard watching my daughter destroy herself. I wasn't mad at Laura; I didn't love her any less or blame her for anything. I was just letting them know how bad it was especially any newcomers at the meeting. They all knew where I was; I was exactly where all of them were or would be. We were all in same boat, and that's why you go to meetings like Nar-Anon: to share and for friendship as well as compassion. You're not going there to have them fix you or your loved one; you're there to help yourself and get well so you can live. This disease will kill you if you let it. Not only can it kill your loved one, but it can kill you as well. That's how strong it is. It will drag you down and take you to places you never though you would see or go to. You may even find yourself self-medicating to deal with the pain. It's like a cancer inside of you trying to destroy you as well.

After two days, I called Retreat to find out how Laura was doing. I was very anxious as normal when it came to Laura being in another rehab. They told me that she was doing well and assured me not to worry; she would be fine. Well, that's easy for them to say because I knew Laura, and at any given time, things could change and she could want out or just leave.

After 12 days, I received a call from her therapist, and I was able to find out everything that was happening and how she was coping in their facility. Laura, according to her therapist, was really opening up about everything and was very talkative. I was really happy to hear that, and very surprised to hear that because Laura didn't really open up about anything related to her or her feelings. This was some positive info that she was telling me, and she also put Laura on the phone, so that all three of us could talk. Laura sounded pleased to be there, and I did not hear anything negative from her. I did believe that she was connecting well with her therapist and actually liked her. I finally felt like there might be some hope that Laura would get the help she needed and not shut down or look to get out.

I told Laura that I would come to see her as soon as I was allowed. We ended our conversation on a positive note, and I would see her soon.

All went well, and I was somewhat relieved. I was trying to stay positive and not get my hopes up because as I have said many times before, things could change real fast with Laura.

That coming weekend, I went to see Laura. I drove close to two hours to Lancaster, traveling up the Pennsylvania Turnpike. It was all rural and farmland made up of mainly homes and farms belonging the Amish. It was a very safe country-like setting.

I checked in the main lobby and waited for them to have a Laura brought to see me. After waiting for a while, I finally saw Laura come through the main hallway. I was so happy to see her, and I hugged her tightly, just as I did in the past during her other stays in rehab. She looked great because she was detoxing up from all the drugs she had used. She had a beautiful smile on her face; a smile that could light up a room. I always knew Laura had a beautiful smile, but she really didn't smile much because of all her problems and her addiction. Laura was a beautiful person, both inside and out. Anyone who really knew her saw this in her.

We sat down in the sitting area that they had for visitors and their family. We spoke about her time there in the last two-and-a-half weeks. She told me that she felt good and was doing well with the treatment program. She again told me that she liked her therapist and was really opening up to her, as well as sharing in her group meetings. This was all great news and positive steps towards recovery. She missed home, but she told me that she wanted to get better and get the help she needed, so she could come home.

After visiting with her over an hour, I knew it was time to leave. I didn't want to stay too long and have her feel homesick or want her to leave or walk out. Here again, this was always difficult to leave her, just as I'd done several times before. I knew in my heart this was never going to be easy or get easier, regardless how many times I would have to do this. I hated it every time, but I really didn't have a choice.

As I drove back home, the sadness just overwhelmed me for the life that Laura had and was given. She was suffering as well as I was suffering with her, leaving her in the hands of people that I didn't even know. But as a parent, what else could I do? I knew I had to push forward and be strong for myself and especially for her.

After four weeks, Laura was now done with residential living and staying on the grounds of the rehab. She was now moved to a sober living house with other girls. She would attend meetings and group meetings at the house. She would be expected to find part-time work, go to clinic each day, attend house meetings, and also go to AA meetings outside of the house as well. It was lot, but they wanted to keep them busy so they didn't have the urge to use. I thought this was a good idea since too much time on their hands or too much down time can lead to trouble, especially for Laura.

The house was a big, beautiful home with plenty of surrounding land. Each girl shared their room with another, and there were five bedrooms with four bathrooms in total.

One day after two weeks of Laura living at the SLH, I got a phone call from Laura. She was extremely upset and crying. It seemed that one of the girls Laura was sharing a room with overdosed on drugs she bought and used. The girl had gone to a meeting the night before along with Laura and then met someone who she got the drugs from. She had died during the night in her sleep and was found dead by the other girls who had tried to wake her up that morning. I was really upset myself when I heard all this and reached out to the property manager as well as the owners of the SLH. They all assured me that they would do whatever it took to see that everyone was taken care of with counseling or whatever else was needed, and this wouldn't happen again even though everyone is drug tested every two days.

I knew Laura would not do well with all this and what had just happened. I feared she would want to come home and not want to stay there anymore. So we talked about it, and I had her therapist work with her about her trying to stay. She finally agreed to stay and work through it all, just as the other girls were doing.

Several weeks had now passed of all that had happened at the house, and I was even going each week to see Laura and make sure she was okay. One weekend while I was there, Laura told me that she had asked to be moved to a different house. She wanted to live in the city part of Lancaster. It was very difficult to find a job where she was living, especially if you didn't have a car to get to and from work. Some of the girls who were living at the house did have cars and others didn't. There was no public transportation because it was in a rural area.

I was okay with her wanting to move as long as it was okay with her therapist and the others at clinical. They okayed her move, and the next weekend I helped Laura move to her new SLH. I didn't really care for the house and the area because it was small and like a row house, but this is what Laura wanted, so I thought, *Well, okay, let's try it.*

The next week was Laura's birthday, so my wife and I drove up to be with Laura on her birthday and take her out to celebrate her special day. I found a really nice Italian restaurant online and called to make reservations. Laura enjoyed the food she ordered and loved the cannoli cake I ordered for her without her knowing of it. They even sang "Happy Birthday" to her with a candle in the cake. I was so glad I could do that for her; I just wish she could have been home to celebrate her birthday like most teenagers her age do. But this was not in the plans for her life; not yet at least. Laura was so happy that we were there for her birthday and as I always told her, "I wouldn't have missed it for the world."

She began looking for work once she got settled in, and there were shops and restaurants nearby as well as a bus line that took you throughout the city. After over a week went by, she wasn't having any luck in finding work and was getting very frustrated and losing hope. I told her to hang in there and give it time. She told me she was getting pressured by the house manager to find a job. Everyone was expected to get a job in the SLH and keep up with their meetings, as well as do clinical and do their house chores. I again reached out to the property manager and the SLH owner who owned this house as well as the other house Laura had come from. They assured me that they would work with Laura and told me that they were not putting pressure on her, but yes, everyone needed to work or be out of the house in the day. They didn't want anyone to be hanging around doing nothing unless it was their day off from work. They wanted you have responsibility and to maintain your schedule and all that was required of you. Laura saw this as a threat and didn't do well with it. She felt this was setting her up for failure. I encouraged her to hang in there and not put so much pressure on herself.

In the coming week, I received a phone call from the house manager telling me that Laura had left, and they didn't know where she had gone. She didn't tell them anything and just took her belongings and left, so of course, I was very fearful now of where she could be or where she was. I knew she had made friends with the house across the street that was a SLH for men. I knew she was close to a guy who was the same age as her living in the SLH there. She talked about him and how they had so much in common and all that he was going through with his add-iction, but I didn't know if she left with him or not. I didn't know what to do but knew she had her phone, so I started calling and texting her, hoping I would be able to get in touch with her or have her reach out to me from where she was. But I wasn't able to get her and didn't hear from her until the next day when she called me asking if I could come and get her. She was staying at some friend's house there in Lancaster. She wouldn't tell me much about who he was or how she knew him. I knew Laura al-ways had a way of connecting with others through social media, and that always worried me, as I'm sure it would any parent. As I said before, when you're on the information highway, social media websites, anything is possible. I told her that I would be there as soon as I could and told her not to leave where she was staying. She texted me the address, and off I went.

After close to about an hour-and-a-half drive, I made it to the address that she gave me. I called her on her phone and told her I was outside and for her to come out. She came out with her bag and all belongings. My wife had also come with me, so we both got out and helped her in the car. She was very intoxicated and was really out of it. I told her she would be fine now and that we would take her home.

She fell asleep for a little while as I was driving but then needed me to pull over because she was going to be sick and needed to throw up. I pulled over on the side of the road, and she left the car to throw up in the grass. I felt really bad and yet upset with her because of what she did to herself. Not to say that she had control over it because I knew she didn't. I knew the addiction once again won.

When we got home, Laura went right up to bed, and I knew she would be sleeping for the next day if not more. I wasn't going to get many answers from her until she was sober, and time was the only remedy for that.

After the following day, I sat down with her and talked about what happened. She explained to me how she just couldn't deal with all the pressure and how her anxiety just won over her body. She needed to self-medicate in order for her to feel better and to overcome what she was dealing with. She knew the meds she had been prescribed weren't going to help her, so she turned to her own healing, which was always drugs and alcohol. I again explained how I felt and how she wasn't going to win this addiction unless she became obsessed with wanting to beat this. It was her battle, not mine. I couldn't do any more for her unless she wanted it so bad that she would win this fight over the addiction.

She wanted to continue with meetings and looking for work. Of course, she was committed to obeying my rules, and she knew them so well because of me always reminding her of them.

The next year brought many ups and downs for Laura. To say that her life took a turn for the better would be lying. It only got worse, and she was consistently spiraling out of control.

She had taken her mom's car one night after her mom went to bed. She drove it into the ghettos of Trenton seeking drugs. She smashed it and left it in a parking lot, then got a ride home from a Good Samaritan. A woman in a minivan saw her walking the streets and was nice enough to drive her home to my house. I then had to go and retrieve her mom's car the next day.

She was arrested several times, once in our township for possession of marijuana and other drug paraphernalia.

She was also arrested for shoplifting in northern New Jersey. She was sent to jail and spent several days there. I will never forget seeing my daughter wearing an orange jumpsuit, standing in front of the judge in the courtroom; a father's worst day to witness his daughter in handcuffs in court. Yet Laura didn't break down or cry while she stood there listening to the judge read off her charges. She had become numb to her life and everything that happened in it, along with every dark road it took her down.

The judge ordered her to pay her bail and seek treatment, so once again, she entered another treatment facility. After speaking to her mom and Nar-Anon, they suggested a treatment facility in Pennsylvania called Livengrin Foundation, located in Bensalem about a 40-minute drive from where we lived.

The following day, I started making all the arrangements in getting her admitted. After they did an insurance check and spoke to Laura, they informed us she was cleared to go as soon as we could get her there.

Laura wanted to see her mom first before she left as well as her current boyfriend. She was buying time and really didn't want to go, but she had no choice. It was either that or possibly go back to court and even jail again. After several hours of stalling and taking her time in getting ready to go, I finally got her in the car, and we left. We got there at almost 9:00 at night only to find out that she forgot her ID, so I had to run back home and get her ID while she did her intake with their staff. When I got back, she was all done with the intake process and was going to be taken to her room. We then said our goodbyes, and I told her as always I loved her and I would talk to her soon.

When I went to the car, I opened the back door where she had her suitcase and her other belongings, and I noticed on the floor a very small bag of what looked to be what drugs would be placed in, usually a powered form. I pretty much knew that she had used, probably in their bathroom before her intake. This is very common of addicts to use before they go for treatment or for detox. Laura had done this before, and I had thought she might this time as well. 'It was her way of being able to cope with going for treatment or her knowing that this would be her last chance to use once she was admitted for treatment.

Laura ended up staying for a total of 12 days at Livengrin before going to a SLH in New Jersey. She would spend the next month going to clinic and working the program. I provided for Laura to live there once my insurance stopped paying. SLHs are not covered once you are downgraded to outpatient (OP). Many SLHs have a clinical program that is also required of you while you live there.

Laura only stayed a total of seven weeks here before she left one day with guy friend she met while living there. I was notified by phone that she had left and had to go and retrieve all of her belongings. It was just expected anymore of her to not stay in one place long before she would want out or a change. She couldn't commit to any place long enough to feel better and to get better. I was always finding myself holding on to hope and prayer, but that was not working for me. I was just feeling more and more stress each time she left. I didn't even know it was possible to feel so low and so hopeless. But again, I would have to remind myself that I wasn't the victim here; she was.

Several days had passed before I heard from Laura. She wouldn't tell me much except that she was okay and was with a friend. She then called me the next day telling me that she was going to live with another guy friend she knew at his aunt's house. I really didn't know what to think except that this is not what I wanted, but I had no control over her. I would always tell her about my concerns and my worries over her and her choices. That's all I could do as her father since she was over 18 now, and she was an adult to make her own decisions and choices.

The following week, I learned that Laura along with the guy friend she was living with at the SLH committed a theft. They went into a fitness health club and stole wallets and car keys from the locker room. They were using and high at the time and needed money, so they used the stolen credit cards to buy needed goods at convenience stores in the area. They were on cameras both at the health club and in a convenience store. The police now were looking for them, and they were wanted for theft, credit card fraud, and other crimes. I called Laura and told her to turn herself in before things got worse for her. She wouldn't listen to me and was afraid I would have to turn her in. I told her if she didn't, I would; I couldn't protect her, and it was just a matter of time before the police found her. I really didn't want to call the police and tell them I knew where she was, but I knew I had to. I had told her that I would give her two hours, and if she didn't call the police, then I would. I found myself praying to God for strength and for Him to show me the way. I loved her so much and just wanted to save her as always, but I was just fooling myself on this.

My mind kept racing on what to do and how could I help her. I was running out of time because I gave her a window of two hours, and I knew I had to hold to this, otherwise she would never believe in me and would use this to her advantage both now and later. I was desperate, and I needed help.

Then the phone rang. It was a number I didn't recognize. I answered it, and it was Laura calling from the police station. It seems someone called and turned her in. She was working at a diner, and the police went there to arrest her. She knew that I didn't turn her in but she wouldn't tell me who did. She wanted me to help her post bail, but I was firm and told her I couldn't. I needed her to suffer the consequences for her actions and take responsibility for her crimes. She was crying and was really upset, but I told her again I couldn't. I was faced again with such a hard decision and hated every minute of it. I just kept thinking how much more pain must I endure in watching my daughter ruin her life even more. When would this night-mare end and when would I get my daughter back? The little girl I raised who was perfect in every way. She was my gift from God and was the greatest miracle I could have ever asked for.

I knew Laura wouldn't call her mom because she knew that her mom would turn her down as well. I think Laura always knew I was the soft one and she could have her way with me—or at least try to.

Laura spent close to five days in the county jail until her friend's aunt she was living with put up her bail. She did call me from jail letting me know all this. I felt really bad, but I couldn't help her. When she made bail, she went back living at her friend's house and continued to look for work again until her court hearing.

Her mom and I discussed hiring an attorney to help her get the help she needed rather than just be thrown back in jail and not get any help for her addiction. We felt that the judicial system would just fail her, as it does so many with addiction problems as well as mental and behavioral problems. So we hired an attorney to plea her case and help with all her outstanding arrest warrants. I knew it would be looked at as if we were enabling her, but I was more concerned with getting her help for her problem of addiction, which again is a disease. I really didn't care who would be judging me at this point. I just wanted her to get the help she deserved and needed. I had always felt this way, and I stood by my decision.

After several months of court hearings and standing in front of a judge, Laura's attorney was able to get her into the Pretrial Intervention Program (PTI), which would keep her out of jail and allow her to get help for her addiction. She also was given two years' probation, to which she would be assigned a probation officer and would be required to meet with her or him on a regular basis.

I allowed her to live with me for a while and helped her with her probation obligations that she had to attend every other week. She really didn't want to live with me, so she ended up leaving and moving in with a girlfriend. She told me she would look for help with her addiction problem and was even thinking about going back to Florida, but she didn't want to go there alone.

She also became involved with her girlfriend's brother, who was dealing with his own addiction problem as well—not the best of news to hear being it's so much harder to help each other when both suffer with addiction; but that was something that Laura didn't want to hear from me or agree with. She felt they would have each other, and it would make it easier for her to overcome her addiction.

Laura wasn't doing well living with her friends. She didn't really work much and couldn't keep a job, just like in all the other previous years of her life. I would drop off food for her from time to time since she didn't have much money to buy groceries and other needed goods. She would always ask me for money, but I had to limit that, for I knew it would only be used to get high.

After several months of Laura living with her friends, she decided her and her new boyfriend would go to Florida and find a rehab that would take them both. Laura was very good at finding what she needed and wanted. And sure enough, she was able to find a rehab in Florida that would take them both. With the help of her mom and a friend who she knew who was involved with placing those who needed help in recovery, she and her boyfriend left for Florida. They went to Palm Beach Shores at Reliance Treatment Center. The rehab paid for both their flights and for transportation once they arrived in Florida. They would now both have to be separated as they did their detox before they could start their recovery. This is how it always is in any treatment center, first detox—whether it's on site or somewhere else—and then the treatment starts after detox is completed. Detox can be anywhere from several days to a week depending on what drugs or other substance was being used and taken.

I would have to wait for Laura to contact me. Since she was an adult now, I couldn't just call the facility and see how she was unless she signed a release form for me, granting me permission to talk to their staff. I did end up calling Laura and tried to find out what was going on; if she was there and was admitted and so on... But I wasn't able to reach her. I then called her mom, who told me what was going on with both Laura and her boyfriend. It seems they made it there to Florida but hadn't check in yet at Reliance Treatment Center. They were walking the streets in Delray Beach, possibly looking to use before going in for treatment. Her mom then called her friend she knew who was is some way connected and who had recommended Reliance. He was living in Florida and knew the area well and set out to find them and take them to Reliance. After several hours, he was able to find them and take them to treatment. We did, however, find out that they got robbed on the streets as they were walking, doing God knows what. They were okay, but here again, this could have turned out really ugly being that far away from home and being in an area that may have not been safe, especially if you're looking to purchase drugs. I was relieved to hear that they were now on their way to treatment thanks to this individual that Laura's mom knew.

Laura was able to reach out to me after two weeks because she needed some personal things and needed me to put money on the books. This is the way that most rehabs and detox facilities offer their clients the ability to purchase goods while they are there.

Some sober living homes also do this, which I have plenty experience with this because Laura was in many so far. Even though she was there with her boyfriend, you could never tell with Laura what was really going on inside her head or what her long-term goal was.

After several weeks, Laura contacted me telling me that she found a better treatment center and felt this would be a better move for the both of them. She was now going to London Treatment Center in West Palm Beach, Florida. It seems she did her research along with discussing it with her boyfriend, and the two of them now were moving on. She was approved by my insurance and was now transitioning over to this new rehab/treatment facility.

I really didn't know what to think as far as her and him moving to a different rehab. I did feel that it was better for the two of them to be in treatment rather than living on the streets.

I couldn't control what she was going to do, but here again, I just wanted the best for her and for her to get the help that she needed so desperately. I really wasn't thrilled that her boyfriend was there, and I wasn't thrilled that he got a scholarship and that he wouldn't have to pay anything, but in all actuality, he was just piggy banking off Laura and my insurance. That's how these scholarships work and are designed to use others' insurance to grant he or she free treatment at most rehabs. I have explained this to a greater detail towards the end of this book.

For the next two months, Laura and her boyfriend were now living at an offsite apartment managed by London Treatment. They were doing very well with treatment and staying sober each day. They both had over 60 days of being clean. They were doing clinical three times a week with London and doing outside meetings as well. Somehow, they were making it work.

I was very happy to hear this and see it myself. I had flown down twice to see Laura while she was there at the London Treatment Center. I had even met with her therapist and discussed her progress in the program they had her in. She was doing well and had a really good attitude with everything and everyone.

The next week, I got a call from Laura telling me that they had to leave their apartment where they were living because they were told that London was closing. It seems that they were being investigated due to insurance fraud and the filing of wrongful claims. I couldn't believe this, so I called and spoke to Laura's therapist who told me the same. She then told me that she would try to place them at another rehab treatment facility in the area, but she didn't know if she could get both in or get Laura's boyfriend accepted into a scholarship program.

Both Laura and her boyfriend now had leave and go stay at a hotel until they could find another rehab that would take them both. I ended up paying for several days and her boyfriend's parents did the same.

I knew this was going to get expensive if they couldn't find another rehab soon, and Laura was now telling me that her boyfriend wanted to go back home for other reasons. She wanted to stay and didn't want to come home with him. I was actually shocked that she wanted to stay and not come home with him. After two weeks of living in a hotel, her boyfriend made plans to leave and go back home to his parents' house. At this point, I needed Laura to get back into a rehab since I was pretty sure they both had been using now even though she told me they weren't. By no means could I rely on her telling me this, so I needed her to either come home or go into treatment again.

Within a week, Laura was able to check herself in to Proactive Treatment Center in Delray Beach, Florida. She was by herself now since her boyfriend left to go back to New Jersey. She was determined to stay in Florida and try to adapt to this new rehab. She would be living with all girls in her SLH and would attend the clinical part of treatment every day, just as in all the other facilities she had gone to.

After a month, Laura left Proactive, claiming it was riddled with drug use and they really didn't care about helping those who were there for treatment. She left and was staying with a guy she knew and considered only as a friend. I wasn't too pleased to hear this, but here again, as I had said before over and over, it wasn't my decision nor my life. I could only try to guide her through all her choices and yes, even her bad decisions. I tried to tell her to get back into treatment and not to give up because this was not the answer, living with a stranger she barely knew. But Laura didn't want to hear it and thought it could work out because he wasn't an addict and he could help her stay clean. I knew better, and time would tell it all.

In the weeks to follow, the phone calls started with Laura complaining of how this guy was trying to control her and tell her everything she needed to do and not do. Little did he realize that Laura wasn't a girl you could control or bark out commands to. I even spoke to him on the phone when he was trying to take over her. This was now becoming abuse, and he was using her as well. I told him I wouldn't have this, and I would come down and pull her out of there as soon as possible and call the police on him if needed. I wouldn't put up with it, and if he put on finger on her, it would be over for him. This, I assured him, and he could take it as a threat; I didn't care. He assured me he wouldn't do anything to harm her or ever abuse her in any way.

I told Laura she needed to get out of there and again seek treatment. She told me not to worry because her boyfriend was on his way back to Florida, and they would be going to another rehab once he got there. It seems she was keeping her boyfriend informed of everything she was living through, and he, too, was on the phone with this guy as well, which I was definitely glad to hear that because I didn't want this guy she was living with to think that Laura didn't have loved ones who were looking out for her and would do whatever it took to keep her safe and to protect her regardless of how far we were from her.

Several days later, Laura called me to let me know that her boyfriend was now there, and they were looking to check into Q-Health Treatment Center, located in West Palm Beach. They were both being accepted into their program for treatment and again her boyfriend would be given a scholarship as well for his treatment. And just in case you're wondering how many treatment centers there are in Florida, well, there is an endless amount. You don't have to travel far to find a rehab/treatment facility or detox center in Florida. You just need to figure out what part of Florida you want to be in, and that's pretty much it, because if you have decent insurance, you will be on your way, and they will take care of everything for you. Problem is you really have to do your homework on each place, otherwise you really don't know what you are getting until it's too late.

In the next five weeks, Laura had left Q-Health seeking yet another rehab because Q-Health was trying to encourage her to use, so they could get more billing time from the insurance and get her to stay longer for treatment. It's a way that rehabs keep top billing for their patients as well as keep them at inpatient status rather than dropping them down to a lower care level. It's very common among rehabs that are in it for only the money. You will also hear about some rehabs that offer money up front to a patient to come to their treatment facility. Again, it's all for the insurance money and not the care when these shady rehabs do these kinds of desperate and illegal measures. I really didn't need Laura to tell me about all this even though she did; I had heard of this before and even read about it in the news. It's just really sad to hear about all this, especially when you send your loved one to rehab to get better and seek the help they so desperately need. I had even gone as far as to reach out to management and Laura's therapist to discuss this and what I had learned regarding Q-Health and their doings, but they only denied everything and told me that they don't practice any of those tactics. And they said that Laura was welcome to come back at any time should she change her mind.

I had told Laura from day one that I wasn't too happy with where Q-Health had her living or the neighborhood and its surrounding area. I had, of course, visited her, just like I had done with all the other rehabs she was staying at, and I found that it would be extremely easy to score or buy drugs right out front of her SLH; not a very smart decision or good choice of neighborhood on Q-Health's part to say the least.

The next rehab that both she and her boyfriend were accepted into was Academy Health Solutions, located in Lake Park Florida. She would spend the next three months here. I visited her several times while she was living there and again met her therapist as well as the director of Academy Health Solutions. She was doing very well here with her treatment and had even found a job and was working. She was staying clean and working the program each day. She seemed happy and confident to continue with treatment and in staying clean. Her boyfriend was also working and doing well with his treatment.

As her three-month date approached, I began to get nervous, knowing that Laura could not really go beyond three months without wanting to use. Her internal clock really started to remind her of how bad she was feeling and her need to self-medicate. Also, her anxiety level now was elevated due to not using, and she saw everything as overwhelming. She said that she wanted to take Xanax to help with the anxiety she was now feeling each day. I told her that they wouldn't allow this because it was a controlled substance, and she knew this already. She insisted it would be okay if her therapist gave her the permission. I knew this wasn't going to be possible and that there was no way they would allow it. She didn't want to hear this from me, and she made an appointment with a local doctor to get a prescription of Xanax. I knew this would be the end of her treatment at Academy Health.

Laura ended up having to leave Academy Health Solutions once they knew she was taking Xanax. It showed in her drug test, plus she had broken curfew and had stayed out all night prior to her test.

Her and her boyfriend ended up staying at a local hotel before they booked a flight back home. She would now stay at her boyfriend's parents' home once they were in New Jersey again.

After Laura got settled in living at his parents' home, she started seeing her probation officer on a regular basis. I would drive up many times to take her or give her money for an Uber ride. I knew it was important for her to see her probation officer and not get in any more trouble by missing her scheduled appointments. Her probation officer also had her do community service as part of her obligation to satisfy the court. I was proud of her for doing what she needed to do in order for her to be done with her two-year probation sentence. I just kept telling her that I was here for her and would always help her get her probation all behind her. I always kept my promise to her and was always consistent in helping her in any way that I could. She would always see this in me.

I also made sure she had her meds refilled that she was on from the doctors at Academy Health Solutions. I made sure to take her to the doctors when she needed to see them for whatever reasons. Laura was covered under my insurance for all this until the age of 26, so that wasn't ever an issue.

Laura lived with her boyfriend for over a year in North Jersey, and in that time, I was giving money to help with her expenses to her boyfriend's parents. I felt it was the least I could do since she had a roof over her head that they provided. She was also attending meetings while she was living there and trying to stay clean each day, but it wasn't easy, and sooner or later, she would need to move on from living there. She would tell me that she wanted out from living there and she was finding it so hard to find a steady job or keep one.

She was living in a house were both parents were dealing with their own addictions as well as her boyfriend's sister, who also lived there. So, it definitely was not a healthy environment to be living in, not for anyone, regardless of addictions or not. Laura kept telling me that it was just temporary until she found a place to live or until she was able to go back to another rehab. I knew this was another ticking time bomb ready to go off. It was just a matter of time before this all came to a head.

In March of 2019, after 13 months of living with her boyfriends' parents, Laura decided to go back to Florida for treatment with her boyfriend. She decided to go to Peak Recovery in Boynton Beach, Florida. Her boyfriend's brother-in-law worked there and recommended it because he was doing so well with his recovery and told her she would be in good hands with him working there and he would watch over them.

I felt that maybe this would be a good fit for both of them since they had a connection to help them with whatever they needed or had to deal with; someone they could trust and not be alone through their whole treatment time while they were at Peak Recovery. I felt positive about it for once and that she wasn't alone now in yet another strange rehab a thousand miles away. Even though she was there with her boyfriend, it made me feel at ease knowing there were now two males looking out for her and not just one.

My wife and I met Laura at the airport to say are goodbyes. Even her mother came to wish her good luck and see her off safely. Laura was very nervous and had taken several Xanax to calm her down. She always needed something to go to rehab; it just wasn't possible for her to go unless she was using. Nothing new; just a repeat, as she did with all the other rehabs she went to.

As I mentioned it several times before, it's to be expected for any addict once he or she goes for treatment to be using or under the influence.

I told Laura once again to please call me once she arrived at Peak Recovery, so I knew they got there and were safe. She agreed and said to me not to worry; she would be fine, and it would all work out. My prayers were with her again, and maybe this would be the place that got her better and clean once and for all. I had to have faith and trust in God, for He was the Driver here as always, not me.

After close to four hours, Laura finally called me to tell me they were there and were now going to be admitted. I told her that I would talk to her after her blackout time and that she was going to do this and this would be her last treatment center. I told her as always that I loved her and that she could do it.

After two weeks, I was able to speak to Laura and to her therapist. We went over her treatment plan and the other things pertaining to her time there, like making sure Laura would be in touch at all times with her probation officer. This was very important, and her therapist Jennifer ensured me that this would be taken care of and she would make sure that Laura called her as much as needed so that she wouldn't violate her probation while she was in Florida. Laura sounded great and positive; she loved having Jennifer as her therapist. Jennifer really felt good about Laura, and it seemed that they connected already in yet a short period of time. She told me Laura was very open with her and wanted to be clean and get her life back, no matter what it took. And she really meant, it unlike all the other times she had said this. Jennifer felt she was being true to herself and the others who were there to help her get clean and stay clean. '

It sounded great and promising, but would it happen? I wasn't trying to be negative, but I wanted this so bad for my daughter, and I had been wanting it for years now.

Peak Recovery separated the males and females, giving them their own private residence to live in until they completed their inpatient program (IP). Once Laura completed her (IP), she then would then be downgraded to an outpatient program (OP). The inpatient program usually lasted about three weeks, and the outpatient program could be four to 10 weeks, depending on the progress that was made while you were in OP.

Laura was able to progress to OP after several weeks and was happy to make that move. She now had much more freedom and would be living in a sober living home with other girls. She would be able to find a job and work as long as she still attended classes three times a week at Peak Recovery, found a sponsor, and attended meetings outside of Peak Recovery on a daily basis.

I helped Laura pay for her SLH while she looked for a job. She really wanted to work and had already found a sponsor who had well over a year of sobriety and was a really good fit for Laura. From what Laura told me about her, she was just like Laura when she was actively using and had turned her life around once she got clean. Laura felt close to her and had a great connection with her as well. I was really happy to hear this because Laura never wanted to work the 12 steps of the program—or even get a sponsor for that matter—so this was a huge step in the right direction. I was so proud of Laura and all the accomplishments she was making now at Peak Recovery. It definitely felt and looked like her life was making a change in the right direction.

Laura wanted me to meet her sponsor the next time I came down to visit, and her sponsor wanted to meet me as well since Laura talked so much about me to her. I felt good about that because I was always trying to help Laura, and now her sponsor was well aware of all I was doing for Laura. I wasn't looking for any praise or acknowledgement; I was just happy and content to hear Laura talking about me to others. I've said this before, it's always important to have someone care, love, and support you when you're an addict; I can't say that enough.

It didn't take Laura that long to find a job. She was offered a waitress position at a restaurant that was known to hire those who were dealing with addictions. It seemed that the owner was giving back to those who needed work and were in the program to get help and stay clean. She would have to be drug tested first before getting the job, which was fine with her because she was tested every couple of days at Peak Recovery as it was. Within the next week, Laura was working and fulfilling all of her requirements both at Peak Recovery and that of her SLH.

She wasn't really involved that much with her boyfriend anymore since he, too, was now living at a men's SLH and was also working. I was happy to hear this because they needed to work on their own recovery separately and not together. This was more good news as far as I was concerned.

Laura now had completed two months at Peak Recovery and was doing well with everything, her treatment and working with her therapist, her job and working the 12 steps with her sponsor. She finally was making great progress in her life and its direction. She was happy where it was taking her, and she was seeing all the possibilities that existed for her now.

I had visited her twice now since she had been at Peak Recovery, and both times, I'd met with her therapist Jennifer as well with the house manager at her SLH. Laura even showed me her room and the rest of the house. She was sharing a room with the house manager, with whom she had become close friends. Her room was organized and neat, which was not the typical way Laura usually kept her room while she lived with me or her mom. She was living a totally different way now, and all for the better. I knew she could see this now, especially being she was clean, and her brain wasn't cloudy or hindered by the drugs when she was using. Unfortunately, I wasn't able to meet with her sponsor because she was working each day, but I knew I would be back again to see Laura, and hopefully, I would meet her then.

I only stayed several days in Florida visiting Laura and taking her out and spending time with her. I would always take her shopping for food, clothes, or anything else she needed while I was there. I also made sure she had an Uber gift card to get back and forth to work. I didn't want her walking home late at night from her job even though it wasn't that far from her SLH. I always made sure Laura had a ride home from work when she was working late; otherwise, I would be worried about her not getting home. Plus, I would never go to bed unless I knew she had a ride home or heard from her telling me that. That's the father I was and would always be, regardless of her age.

Time to say my goodbyes, I knew I would be back again soon, so I was okay with this even though I hated it when I had to say goodbye. It was never easy, and I just wished I lived in Florida, so I could be there to see her all the time. I remember when Laura told some of her friends at Peak Recovery when she introduced me to them that I was going to be moving there, and they were so kind and happy to hear that I would be living there in Florida close to Laura. That made me feel really good as well as how it made Laura feel, wanted and not alone.

The next day, I said my goodbyes to Laura in the driveway of her SLH. I hugged her tight and told her how proud I was of her and to keep it going. She was doing it, and she could do this. As always, I told her that I loved her and believed in her. I left with tears in my eyes and anger. I was upset as always to why Laura; why God couldn't save her and for her to be done with her addiction forever? I was always dealing with this in my head, and it was just always there, especially when I would visit Laura at all the different rehabs and SLHs. As I would always say to myself to help with being so angry about all of it: *Just give it to God, Anthony, and move on.*

In the next couple of weeks, I scheduled another trip to fly down and see Laura. She needed to see a dentist because she hadn't seen one or had a yearly checkup in well over a year. I found a dentist in the area where she was living and scheduled the appointment. I made sure she would be off, so that I could take her.

That coming weekend, I flew down to see Laura and would stay a total of three days to take her to the dentist and anywhere else she needed. She had seen her new general practitioner I had taken her to during my last trip down and had gotten her renewal scripts for her meds that she was taking daily. I always tried to get everything done while I was there visiting Laura that couldn't be done without me being present. It's never easy trying to do these things when you're a thousand miles away. This, I know so well now, and this is why I made the best of my time while I was with her because, once I left, I knew she and I would be limited to what we could get done. Plus, Laura didn't have a car, so that really made it difficult for her to get around. Also, she had limited money and couldn't afford a lot of things since her paycheck was that of a waitress, which, as you know, is always different and changing. It's not a nine-to-five salary job; not at all. This is why I was always helping her with money regardless of whether she was working or not because I knew there was no way she could make it or survive without my help. And yes, I was always aware of not trying to enable her, but that was a fine line as we all know.

That Monday, I took Laura to the dentist and had them do a complete checkup as well as a cleaning. I waited for her in the waiting room while she saw the dentist. After about an hour, she came out and said that the dentist wanted to talk to me. I went in and met with her dentist, and he began to go over her checkup and cleaning. He proceeded to tell me that, in examining her teeth, he saw in her x-rays that her wisdom teeth needed to come out; they were growing into her other teeth. He told me that this would cause other problems as well as her having a lot of pain if they were not taken out. I really wasn't expecting this since that Laura was not complaining about her teeth at all. He showed me the x-rays, and I could see how her wisdom teeth were growing every way except straight up. This was not good at all. He explained that he could take them out in his office and she would have very little discomfort from the extractions. He would then give her some medication for the pain. I then explained that she could not take pain medication and asked if there was anything else she could have instead. He replied only Tylenol or Motrin.

I remember when I had my wisdom teeth taken out; I had all four of them taken out as well, and I was sick in bed for a week with a lot of swelling and pain. This was not good news at all and not what Laura needed to hear.

We decided to let the dentist know once Laura knew what her schedule would be and when she would be off for several days, so she could have time to rest and heal. Laura was really upset and worried about all the pain she would have and not be able to take anything for it. I just keep assuring her that it would be fine and I would come down and stay with her as long as it took for her to be well again. She knew of others who had it done and said they experienced a lot of pain from having them taken out. I told her everyone is different and to not listen to others and what they tell you. I told her she would be fine and not to worry about it because she wasn't going to be alone in all this.

I took Laura to Walmart to get some things she needed and then took her to dinner. She wasn't acting the same because of what the dentist told her, and I could see she was worried, especially about the pain and not being able take anything for it. I felt so bad for her, and I just wanted to fix everything for her as always. I wish it was me who needed them taken out even though I did have them removed already. I just hoped she would be able to deal with all this because she was now coming up on 90 days of being clean. This could throw her off and make her want to use. She had never done 90 days, so every day was difficult and a real challenge for Laura, sponsor or no sponsor.

Also, in the beginning of sobriety, the addict will go through what they call clouding, or pink cloud syndrome, which involves the feelings of euphoria and elation, like "Everything is good," and "I can do this." But it usually doesn't last long, and the addict then begins to crave or struggle once again to use.

I was leaving the next day to go back home and would have to say my goodbyes in the morning before I went to the airport. I took Laura back to her SLH and told her I would see her in the morning before going to the airport.

That morning, I got dressed and packed and headed over to see Laura to say my goodbye's. I got to her SLH and texted her that I was there in the driveway and waited for her to come out. She came out after several minutes and looked better, not overcome with fear like yesterday. She told me that her roommate and house manager had hers taken out several years ago and that she would take care of Laura when she had hers done. I thought this was the nicest thing I could hear, and Laura was very fortunate to have a roommate like her. I told her that I still would come down for as long as she needed me to and that she was in good hands for sure now since she had someone who really cared about her right there living with her. I felt much better knowing this.

I hugged and kissed her tight and gave her an extra hug for her mom, who would always ask me to do this for her. I told her I love her and that everything was going to be fine and it would all work out; there was nothing for her to worry about. With tears in my eyes, I left her there in the driveway and got in my car to drive to the airport. I wasn't too upset this time because I would be back in less than a week. Laura didn't know this, but I had planned this trip a while back and would be coming this time with Helen. I wanted to surprise her and didn't want to say anything yet. I knew she would love the surprise once she heard I was back in Florida.

In the next couple of days, I kept texting Laura, making sure she was okay and told her to let me know what her schedule was like so that we could set a date with the dentist to have her wisdom teeth taken out. I didn't want it to go to long, otherwise she might change her mind and not have it done, plus this really needed to be done sooner than later.

On June 7, I spoke to Laura several times that day. She was upset because someone in her house had taken some of her things the day before. This was common and happened to her before. Some girls come with nothing and have nothing, so they take from the other girls. It's not tolerated in any SLH, and you can be thrown out for stealing. I assured Laura that they would catch the person and to let it go. I told her I would replace what was taken. She told me that wasn't the problem; she just hated the fact that people would steal from her. I reminded her that everyone steals when they're an addict, including her, whether they're clean or not. It happens, but I was sorry it happened to her more than others. I also reminded her that she has some nice things I had bought her, and I'm sure other girls are jealous of her possessions. She finally understood and started to calm down and come to terms with all of it. I told her to have a good night; I said that I loved her as I usually did when I ended my text or call to her. She texted me, *I love you too* and applied an emoji with a kiss. I thought that was really sweet that she did that. It was 9:47 when she sent that.

In less than two days, we would be leaving to go see Laura and to surprise her. I couldn't wait to surprise her with this.

My twin brother was also there in Florida, and I would be meeting him as well, so I was really looking forward to this trip. I love going to Florida, but I loved it more because Laura was there. That's what really made it special. I would always say, "Florida is Laura." And it's where she wanted to be.

That night, I went to bed at my usual time around 11:00 PM and thought of Laura and how I would be seeing her the day after tomorrow. I didn't sleep well, and it took me a while before I could fall asleep, but eventually, I did fall asleep. I tend to sleep harder after 4:00 AM and was awakened by the sound of my front doorbell. At first, I thought I was dreaming, but I also heard the banging on the door. I looked at my clock, and it read 5:47 AM. I and my wife both got up, and my wife looked out the front window and told me she saw a police car outside by our house.

I rushed downstairs and opened the door, and before I could say anything they asked me if I had a daughter named Laura. I said, "Yes, why? What is going on?"

They then proceeded to tell me that she had passed away last night. I said, "What? I just spoke to her last night. That can't be."

They said they got a call from the Boynton Beach Police around 2:00 AM. They had found her body in a motel room unresponsive to where the emergency medical technicians (EMTs) couldn't revive her. I now couldn't believe what I was hearing. My body went numb, and I felt like I was going to pass out. I had to sit down on the stairs and try to breathe and not pass out. I heard my wife saying, "No, this can't be right."

The officers were now standing in my foyer, telling us that I needed to call the number of the detective who was handling the case with the Boynton Beach Police. My mind was spinning out of control, and I wasn't hearing much of what they were saying. I couldn't think or process anything expect that she had died according to the officers in my house. I kept telling myself that this was not real; *She is not dead. She can't be. She has so much life in her and God would not do this to her, or me.*

This had to be a mistake. I did hear them say that her boyfriend was with her and that he went to the hospital they brought her to. They said that it looked to be a drug overdose, but I would have to call the detective assigned to her case. I finally got a piece of paper to take down the detective's phone number as well as a case number. I still remember to this day that the officers had no compassion or feelings in their delivery of what happened to Laura. It's as if they were telling me that my pet had died and that was it. They really didn't want to stay long and wanted out of this as soon as possible. They had no training in any of this, and they seemed to be lost and had very little information to tell me except to call the number they were given. I was just mortified and in shock at this point, with them as well as the whole situation.

After the officers left, I knew I had to compose myself and stop the crying and the uncontrollable shaking. I had to make this call and find out what happened to Laura. My wife was very shaken up and couldn't believe any of it as well. She, too, felt that the officers had gotten it wrong and Laura was not dead. .

I didn't want to make this call, but I knew I had to, so I got the piece of paper with the phone number and made the call. I remember someone answering and I told them the case number as well as the detective's name. After some time waiting, they passed me on to the detective handling Laura's death. Her proceeded to tell me that Laura had overdosed at a motel called the Homing Inn in Boynton Beach. He was very sorry to have to tell me all of this, but she was not alone and was with her boyfriend who was with her the whole time she was there. The detective then told me that he was not using and Laura had fallen asleep with him some time after midnight. He then woke up and realized that she had thrown up and that she wasn't breathing, and she had turned blue. He then called 911 and waited for the police and EMTs to come. The EMTs tried to revive her, but it was too late; she had already passed. The detective felt she must have died sometime after midnight. He assured me that an autopsy would be performed to find out all the specifics. He also told me that her body was at the hospital morgue, and they would keep it there until arrangements could be made on my end. I told him that I was flying down tomorrow to Florida and I would call him once I arrived.

I knew I had to now call Laura's mom and tell her what had happened. She lived around the corner from me, but it was still very early in the morning, so I decided to wait. I also wanted to call my brother who was there in Florida and tell him. I knew he would go to the police station and find out more details until I could get there tomorrow.

I waited until 8:00 AM to call Laura's mom, hoping she would be awake. Her husband answered the phone and told me that she was still sleeping. I told him not to wake her and then told him that Laura had passed away early this morning. I remember him saying, "No," over and over, again and again. He, too, was in shock of what I had just relayed to him. I then told him I would be coming over to tell Laura's mom and for him to not say anything until I get there.

I once again had to compose myself and try to be strong to tell Laura's mom that our daughter, our only child, was no longer with us. How was I supposed to do this? I kept asking God to please help me, for this is the worst day that any parent could face. This was so wrong. A child should never die before their parents. It goes against all the principles of life and its meaning.

My wife and I walked over to her house, which as I stated earlier was just around the corner. It now was after 8:00 AM, and I felt like I was up for days now. I was psychically and mentally drained and well as weak. I rang the doorbell, and Laura's stepdad answered the door. He told us to come in and that he would go and wake up Laura's mom. I remember saying, *Please, God, give me the strength to do this and to be strong.*

After what seemed to quite a while, Laura's mom came out into the living room and ask why I was there. I couldn't speak at first but then I started to tell her that Laura had passed away sometime after 12:00 AM and the police had come to the house early this morning to inform me of her passing. I really didn't know how else I could word it. I just tried to be honest and direct.

She looked at me as though she didn't hear me or was numb to what I told her. She was composed at first and was keeping it all together, but the tears soon were running down her face. She wanted to know what happened and was looking for details of her passing. I tried to give her as much information as I had and told her what the officers had relayed to me when they came to the house earlier. I also informed her that I would be leaving for Florida tomorrow and would know more once I got there. I made sure she knew that I would keep her informed as much as I could once I learned more of how and where she died. My wife Helen was very supportive of her as well as her husband. She understood what she was facing with the loss of her daughter. It was a very delicate and difficult time now for both of us. We knew both of us were at a loss and shared the pain together even though we were not married anymore. Losing your only child is debilitating as well as devasting whether you are married to this person or not. It goes without saying that we were both now suffering and filled with pain because we had just lost our daughter Laura.

I couldn't sleep at all that night; I just wanted to get to Florida and seek the answers of her death as well as make all the arrangements to get Laura back home for a proper burial. I got up that morning very nervous and anxious to get going and get to Florida as fast as possible.

We finally arrived in Florida that afternoon, and we waited for my brother Joseph to get to our hotel. He arrived not long after we checked in, and we embraced and cried in the parking lot for a while. He was there with his partner David, and he, too, was crying as we all embraced each other over the loss of Laura.

We then went inside and sat in the seating area within the hotel lobby and talked about what our next course of action would be. I really couldn't think straight, so having my twin there was a Godsend, as was my wife. He explained to me how he went to the Boynton Beach Police Department and spoke to the detective in charge already and told him who he was and that he needed to know what happened to his niece. This saved me a trip as well as a lot of anxiety in having to meet with the detective and go over all the details of Laura's death. Plus, there was no way I would be able to process any of this now; I was in no shape or form to handle any of that.

My brother suggested to me that we should go and make the necessary funeral arrangements at a funeral home there in Boynton Beach. This way, the funeral director could go and have her body released from the morgue at Bethesda Hospital in Boynton Beach. I agreed with this and knew it had to be done sooner rather than later. My brother was well equipped in this kind of decision making. He took care of all this for both of my parents when they had passed. He made sure they had burial plots purchased way before their deaths, something many of us don't think of until that time arrives.

Before we were to go, my brother wanted to give me something he purchased for me: a gift that would remind me both of Florida and Laura. He gave me a designer bracelet that was blue and made of fine woven leather. The blue was that of the clear Florida ocean waters. This was so beautiful and so special. It would always remind me of Laura and how she loved the blue Florida waters and beaches. I knew I would always treasure this and remember it, but especially who gave it to me, my twin brother.

We gathered ourselves and our belongings and got into my brother's car and headed to the funeral home in Boynton Beach.

We met with the director of the funeral home, who took down all the information regarding Laura and her death. It was extremely difficult for me to try to remember all the information and details that he was asking. My mind was blank, and I couldn't think or focus. But between my brother and my wife, they were able to supply him with everything that was needed, so he could take care of all the arrangements to get Laura back home. He assured me that everything would be taken care of, and he was extremely kind and caring. I was so grateful for him being this way and for being a God-sent person that he was, especially considering the business he was in as well. He told us to come back tomorrow so we could see her before she was to be sent to Fort Lauderdale in Florida for cremation. I was beside myself thinking about coming back tomorrow having to deal with her body and viewing it.

We left the funeral home and decided to get something to eat. I wasn't really hungry, but I knew I needed to eat to keep myself going and to hopefully be focused on everything that would be happening with getting Laura back home. My brother was the solid one along with David. They kept me busy thinking of doing other things and trying to keep me preoccupied while I was there with them. I could always count on my brother; he was a true leader and had a way with people and getting things done. A true blessing that I would always pass on to my mom in my prayers each day.

The next day we headed back to the funeral home to see Laura. I really didn't sleep much due to being so anxious about seeing her. As we arrived at the funeral home, I just knew this was too much for me and that I couldn't go in and see her. I agreed to go in and meet with the funeral director, but I was troubled about what to do. He told me she was all ready for us to see her. I broke down and began crying and shaking, fearing to see her lying there in a casket. I couldn't do it; this was way too much for me. I felt sick and felt like I was going to pass out. My brother knew this and told me not to worry; he would go in for me and tell her I loved her and would see her again. I told him to please tell her I would see her soon, and she was so loved and missed by me. My wife as well as David also went in to see her. I stayed behind in the meeting room by myself, just crying and wondering if I was making the right choice as not to see her before she was to be cremated in Fort Lauderdale. I just couldn't bring myself to do this, and even till this day, I still think about the choice I made and if it was the right choice.

After what seemed like hours, my wife, my brother, and David all returned to the meeting room I was waiting in. They all seemed very composed and calm. They told me that Laura looked so beautiful and was lying there like God's angel. I once again began crying and thanked them all for seeing her and being there for her and for me. I remember my wife telling me that David was saying and reading prayers to her. I will always remember that and what he did for her and me. I am so proud and honored to know David, for he is a truly a remarkable person who I have nothing but respect for. I will always remember that day and what David did for my Laura.

We left Florida after several days of being there, and Laura's ashes would now be sent back to New Jersey. My brother and I made the arrangements with a funeral home that we used for both my parents, which was well known for its warm and compassionate services.

I made sure that Laura would have a Catholic burial and would be laid to rest in Princeton, New Jersey, where both my parents are buried. I know Laura is home now with them, and her pain and sufferings are over.

In Closing

When I look back at all the rehabs, detox, and sober living homes that Laura was at, there were over 15 of them. Some of them, I didn't even talk about or mention in my book. I also didn't talk about all times she was arrested, her arrest warrants or the time she got into a bad car accident because of drug use. It was extremely difficult for me to write about all this and for me to go back in time to describe and remember these horrific times for both Laura and myself. I tried to cover as much of her life as I could and in detail, so you could see all the pain, suffering, and the uncertainty in her life that she had to live with each day.

I want everyone to know that my daughter Laura did not die in vain, nor do I believe any addict does. I will stand up for her and defend her until I'm no longer here on this Earth. Many people chose not to acknowledge her death or acknowledge her parents for the loss of their only child or even to attend her funeral. It's as if they were embarrassed because of the way she lived her life and the way she died. There are also those who would look at me as enabling my daughter because of her addiction ; I look at it as loving her and doing anything and everything in my power to help her, no matter what the cost.

And yet there were those who would talk about her and mention to me how wonderful she was but were never there for her when she could have used a friend, a companion, or someone who cared about her. It makes me extremely sad, and it will sadden me forever knowing that those who called her their friend were not there for her nor did they want anything to do with her because of her addiction. The Bible says we should not judge others, but we all do, especially when it comes to addiction and the way society frowns upon it. It's as if it's a dirty and disgusting habit, with people not realizing it's a disease, not a way of life or the way anyone wants to live their life.

We are told in life to forgive and forget and move on. All very true and all words of God. But can we do this? That is the question. Losing your child and having her forgotten or neglected is a constant memory, and it is so painful to just forgive and forget. For me, it's because she was my daughter, and nothing can replace her, and that will always haunt me because of how others looked at her and thought of her, as well as us, her parents. I know we are all different, and there are those who can forgive and forget as well as move on. I know it is something that I will look to God for and His healing, as I do every day since Laura died.

I also have and live with the memories of how she was so used, abused, and taken advantage of by so many, especially those who dated her and were supposedly her boyfriends. Being a girl with addictions just opens up the world to men/guys who will always look to use you and take advantage of you in the worst possible ways, and you never have the same ability to protect yourself as a male would in any open situation that may come your way or that you are faced with. I live with the knowledge of what was told to me from both from Laura and her therapists in all the different rehabs, as well as others who knew her and what she went through just in her everyday life. No father should have to live and know about how their daughter was treated and taken advantage from so many guys and girls. It just adds to the deep long pain within me.

My beautiful daughter Laura gave me life and a reason to live. She was my joy and the best thing to ever happen in my life. There isn't a day, an hour, or minute that I don't miss her or think about her. I loved taking care of her and providing for her; it truly gave me a reason and was so self-rewarding. I saw my mom do this with her children, so I learned from the best.

I remember the day being on vacation in Florida, lying by the pool and getting a phone call telling me that Laura had left her SLH. I still till this day remember a song that was playing while I got the call. And today, when I hear that song, it takes me back to that day and time when Laura left her SLH. I remember every phone call when she was in trouble or left a SLH, a rehab, or was being arrested. I know I suffer from post-traumatic stress disorder (PTSD). And after many years, I still live with all this. It is just part of my life, and it will always be. It's not a switch that I can just turn off, nor can I delete it from my memory.

I always tried to not idolize Laura and tried to make God my first love as the Bible tells us. But I have to admit that wasn't easy for me to do because Laura was my only child. God gives and takes; our children are on loan to us. They really are not ours forever. We are created by God and given back to God, something that many of us don't realize until our children are taken from us. God doesn't make mistakes when He creates each and every one of us, and our children are no exception to that. And that's what Laura was: She was no mistake but perfect in every way, even with her addiction. She was unique and special in all her ways, and I wouldn't have changed anything about her. I did pray to God every day to save Laura and not to take her, but to take me instead. My prayers, as you know, were not answered. Instead, she was taken and not me. I know that it will always be God's will, not ours. I know this so well after all these years in praying to Him, and I have to believe that all this will be explained to me one day from God, and I do trust Him, for He knows all what is best for us. I may not like it; I may not understand all of this; but I have to believe in Him and trust in Him and in what He gives me. I know Laura was suffering every day with her addiction, so I have to believe God saved her from her continuing pain and suffering. She lived life not knowing where her next rehab or sober living home would be. There was so much uncertainty in her life every day, especially not having a place she could call home because of her addiction. No child should have to bear this or have to live this way and live in fear as well.

I pray for all those parents who have to go through what I did. I struggle every day, just as I'm sure they do also because of losing their child or a loved one. But I do believe that one day, we will all be reunited with our child or children once we have left this life we were given , and I will hold onto this and look forward to that day, for I know that God will bring my Laura back to me and I back to her.

Laura Nicole Varone died in the early morning of June 8, 2019, at the Homing Inn in Boynton Beach, Florida, from an overdose that contained Fentanyl. She was 24 years old. Her body was cremated in Fort Lauderdale, Florida, and her ashes were then flown back to New Jersey. She had a Catholic burial, and she was laid to rest in Princeton, New Jersey. She is buried where both my parents are, and I know she is home with them in God's house and at peace.

I love you and miss you every day, Laura. You will never ever be forgotten.

My Prayer to Laura

Heavenly Father,

I thank You for giving me the greatest miracle that You could have given me, my Laura. I thank You for the time I had with her and all the help You provided for both me and her, for I know I could not have done it without You. Laura was perfect in every way, even with her addiction, for I know You do not make mistakes. May she be enjoying all of heaven and those who are with her. I pray she is with her Nonna, who will take good care of her until I can get there to be with her forever. Lord Jesus, grant me the strength that I need each day to live without my Laura and help me with this broken heart of mine.

Amen.

I shared the following with Laura when she graduated from high school. I wanted her to know all this. She was so touched and told me she was so glad that I shared this with her, and she would always hold on to it.

The Things I Do and Feel that You May or May Not Know About:

- I would always wait in the teachers' parking lot until the bus came to take you to Vo-Tech, just in case it did not come, so I could then take you.
- I would always try to help you straighten up your room and your bathroom.
- I would always try buy and to make the food you liked and wanted to eat.
- I would always try to make sure you were up and ready for school each day.
- I would always try to make sure you were getting enough sleep and going to bed at a decent hour.
- I would always wait up for you when you went out to make sure you were safe and okay when you came home.
- I would always call or text you when you were out to make sure you were okay and that you knew I was there for you.
- I would always try to make sure you felt loved, and you were loved no matter what.
- I would always try to tell you that I cared about you and would never stop caring.
- I would always try to say "I love you," even when you did not want to be bothered or were mad at me.
- I would always encourage you to do your best and never give up on yourself.
- I would always try to tell you how proud I was of you and how beautiful and special you are.
- I have always believed in you, and I will never give up on you.
- I would always try to tell you how great you are doing in school and always built you up.

• After losing my parent's, it was you who gave me the strength to push forward.

• I learned from my mom to take care of your children the best you can and to provide for them always, and this is what I try to do each day for you.

A Letter I Wrote After Laura Passed Away

To my sweet, beautiful Laura,

You were the best thing to ever happen in my life, and I was blessed by God the day you were born, January 24, 1995. I loved you each and every day unconditionally and was so proud of you for all you accomplished.

You added sunshine to my day, even if it was cloudy and raining out. It was never your fault for the problems that you were given and the disease of addiction that you had to battle with each and every day. You had so many unbelievable qualities. You were smart, caring, and very talented at everything you applied yourself at and, of course, just so beautiful. Your smile would always light up the room. And all those who knew you loved you. No one loved you more than I did, and no one believed in you more than I did. I hope I made you happy and that I was a good dad. I really tried to be, and I never gave up on you, no matter what.

I want to make a difference now and make you proud of me, and I hope that you were always proud of me as your dad. I died the day you died, but I know I will see you again. I know I will. Until then, just know you are loved each day and all the days to follow. I hope you will always be with me every day as I am with you. I miss you so much. I love you, my baby Laura, Daddy's girl.

If you or a loved one is suffering from addiction, please get help or try to get them help. Reach out to your local town, county, or state for a listing of Al -Anon, Nar-Anon, Alcoholics Anonymous (AA), Narcotics Anonymous (NA), Cocaine Anonymous (CA), etc. for meetings. Your local church as well as your family physician can also render help. There is also findtreatment.gov that will render help to any addict. This is not a disease that you can do it by yourself or go it alone. There is plenty of help out there. Please do not wait to get help or put it off. Your life matters as well as your loved one's.

Laura Nicole Varone
January 24, 1995 – June 8, 2019

The End

The Insurance System and How It All Works

I've asked myself why so many people have to die because of drug addiction. When will society and the world accept that this is an epidemic? I wish I could make a difference, and I want to make a difference and help so many who are suffering each day. It's why I am writing this book: to help others and educate them on addiction and how it affects not only the addict, but their family and loved ones.

Laura had so much love to give within her. She cared about others and was so giving of herself, her money, her things, etc. Her addiction ruled her life, but it didn't rule her heart. I will always remember that and how, even without any money, she looked for ways to help others. Many didn't know that about her, but I did and would witness it many times. She reminded me of myself and how I always want to help others but get so upset because of not having the funds or the means to help so many who are suffering, so I try to help where I can (or could). That's all I can do and have to accept it.

I also made the promise to myself that I would not stop in trying to close the Homing Inn. I would also reach out to the media if needed, so the whole world would know of the Homing Inn and what goes on there as well as how I lost my daughter to this horrible, disgusting place that is a well-known crime-infested hotel in Boynton Beach, Florida.

There is so much corruption in the world today that it makes people chase money rather than caring about human life. I saw all the corruption and greed firsthand in the detox and rehab centers for addiction; how these centers take in so many young addicts and only to treat them for the addiction, even though they will advertise and tell you that they are a dual-diagnosis treatment facility. It is well-known that you must also treat the mental illness side as well, otherwise the addict will continue to self-medicate and continue to use. Many will argue and tell you that the addition comes first, not the mental illness; others will say, no, the mental illness comes first, otherwise the addict will never have the ability to quit or help themselves. It's almost like giving them no hope if you don't treat the mental illness and why they want to or continue to use. By treating or concentrating on the addiction only, you will have the addict return or fail to get better.

And yes, many rehabs rely on you coming back because it's not always about getting the addict better but about making more money off them and their insurance reimbursements. I even found out that many treatment facilities offer free scholarships. It's how my daughter got her boyfriend to go where she was going. It's known as a piggy-back. What that means is the person with the insurance carries another person, so its two for the price of one: two people being treated using one insurance carrier. That just shows you have much is charged and how much the facility makes on profit from running these treatment centers, and yet they sell it as a free a scholarship. It's not free; nothing is free. It's all for money, otherwise they wouldn't be opened for business. You're led to believe that they really care and they are doing this to help so many addicts by offering these scholarships. These facilities love the young addict, knowing they can make so much money off them and they might return several times to their treatment center alone. It's a pretty good feeling if you're the owner of one of these facilities.

You'll see treatment centers pop up everywhere, and in every state, you will find treatment centers for addiction, especially in the warm-weather states and those states that are close to the ocean. After all, you want to attract the addict to the nice weather and sandy beaches, so they can get better and feel better where they are. It's all a marketing ploy to draw the addict in or to draw their loved one's family or parents in.

There are no limits nor boundaries that these treatment centers will not take. Everything is on the table and will be offered to you. They will promise you the moon to get you to come there. I remember them telling my daughter everything she wanted to hear and lying to her so many times, as well as to me, her father. They made it all sound like she would be fixed and good as new and that I could rest assured there was now nothing to worry about; she was in the best of care with the best of care and staff at their facility; and she had made the right choice by calling them and checking herself in. They always wanted to make sure I knew I could call them whenever to check up on my daughter or talk to her therapist regarding her treatment and her wellbeing. Here again, this was all to make me feel like she made the right choice and I should support her for making that choice. In other words: Keep telling Laura she did the right thing by choosing this treatment center. I always made sure to tell Laura I was proud of her for being in treatment; and I was very proud of her. You have no idea how proud and happy I was that she was seeking help, even if I knew it wasn't the best facility to choose. But I knew she chose it, so that was a huge step for Laura, and what parent couldn't be happy for their child for making that first big step towards getting better and getting help? Remember, recovery is for people who want it, not who need it. And Laura wanted it. She knew it would never work without the want.

I remember when Laura was in one of the Florida rehabs, and she told me that she saw the doctor they assigned to her and she saw him through Skype. She said she was interviewed for her treatment plan and her meds that she would need and be given. I couldn't believe this and was shocked at what she had told me. This was the first time I ever heard of this out of all the rehabs and detox facilities that she had gone to or been in. Usually, the doctor who was assigned to the rehab would visit or see the patient/client in person when needed. Not through Facetime or Skype. So the next day, I called the director at her rehab and asked about this and if this was a normal practice for them to have their doctor Skype with my daughter rather than seeing her in person. They assured me that this was done all the time with each client, and they never had any issues with it or with the service the doctor was providing. I told them that I wasn't really happy about this and I felt my daughter should see a doctor in person, not through Skype.

Later that week, I reached out to my medical insurance to ask them if this was legit and acceptable for both them and for me, who would be billed or sent an Explanation of Benefits (EOB). They assured me that this was legit and is done many times at rehabs, nursing homes, etc., rather than the doctor visiting on site with each patient. They also informed me that the doctor could bill as high as $2,100 for each Skype visit. I told them that was such an injustice and so wrong to do to my daughter or any other induvial. They really didn't want to hear it from me; it's as if I was bothering them with this and all my questions as well as concerns about this rehab and its doctor charging this insane about of money, so I just gave up and came to the conclusion that there was nothing I could do. They, the insurance carrier, had their reasons and rules that they went by, and this was all okay with them, and that was pretty much the bottom line. I feel as if the insurance is in with these rehabs even though they swear that is not the truth or the case. Here I was trying to find out if there is anything I could do to blow the whistle on all these rehabs and detox centers that run such shady facilities that don't provide the services they tell you and advertise on their websites.

Sure, there are some rehabs that are honest and want to treat the addict and get him or her well again; and yes, there are the few who are treated only once and make a full recovery and are able to be remain clean and sober throughout rest of their lives.

But this is not the majority or the norm for most addicts. My daughter was in over 13 detox and rehabs both in New Jersey, Pennsylvania, and Florida. She never got to be in treatment more than 35 days. I was usually told that the insurance wouldn't pay or didn't want to pay, especially after she was in so many different facilities. It was as if they gave up on her; plus the facility didn't really help or try to work with the insurance company and justify her needing more time. Anyone who knows or understands anything about addiction knows that you can't be treated for 30 days and expected to be 100 percent cured. You need at least 90 days in rehab or a treatment facility that deals with addiction in order to be successful in dealing with your addiction. I spent so many endless hours on the phone with my insurance carrier trying to make them understand how my daughter needed more days in rehab. They just didn't understand and or care. They had no idea of what addicts deal with and suffer from. Most addicts feel alone, different, disconnected; they don't fit in and are not loved or wanted. Most of them deal with and have mental illness as well. I can't say that enough. They usually lack self-esteem and will have addiction somewhere in their family or their family history.

Those in the insurance industry or business are programed to look at their rules and regs of what length of time each addict should get while in treatment. They never looked at who my daughter was or her background; she was just a number to them not a name, Laura Nicole Varone. It was beyond frustrating to say the least. Every addict is unique, not just a number or a name associated with that number. And because every addict is different, that needs to be taken into account. You can't just look at what the average addict should get as far as time goes both in detox and rehab. It's just so wrong and despicable.

But that's what they do, and did, each time with Laura. It's as if she was being punished because she would return to treatment time after time, and it was her fault that she wasn't getting better or clean. My daughter never wanted this nor does any addict want this life. No one would want this life, even if you had no addictions in your family or bloodline. No one in their right mind would ever say, "When I grow up, I want to be an addict." But yet here we are with all of this, and the whole world is now dealing with this epidemic even if they choose to be in denial of its existence. It's here, and its only getting worse. The numbers don't lie of the deaths in America from drug use. In 2021, there were 106,699 fatal overdoses; that's over a 292 a day who die from drug addiction.

Fatalities from Fentanyl were 70,601 of the 106,699 deaths.

These numbers have increased from past years and will continue to increase in the years that lie ahead unless action is taken from our government and lawmakers. All this information is public and is from the National Institute on Drug Abuse, www.drugabuse.gov, and the CDC, www.cdc.gov

Americans tend to only react or want change when it affects them. COVID-19 is a perfect example of that. When the

Coronavirus plagued the world in early 2019, everyone got concerned and feared what lied ahead for them and our world. It wasn't until the number of deaths got real each day that Americans and the world wanted answers and help. Should drug addiction be any different than the Coronavirus? Should the world look the other way on addiction until it affects them or many of their family members and friends? Why is it that we as a society don't want to be bothered or get involved until it affects us? Why is our government aware of the '"War on Drugs," and how it is being lost, not won? They will tell you that they are on top of it all and are making changes to stop the drugs that come into our nation and help the young people who are being affected by all of this, but the truth is that they are not even close to slowing down the flow of illegal drugs that come into United States each day.

Our borders are a free-for-all of this. There are so many holes and gaps all along the borders of how the drug cartels can import their product into the streets of America, and that's exactly what they are doing each day to our children and the youth of America. Our government needs to tighten our borders and give the resources that are needed to make this stop or show us that we our winning the War on Drugs. Just as they came up with the resources needed and money to curb COVID-19, they need to do the same here. They can make a difference and address this epidemic rather than looking the other way and try to silence it or deal with it at another time. I know our government faces so many different problems each day that plague our nation, but these are our children of tomorrow. We need them to care today and every day. Can we really just look the other way or sweep it under the carpet until we want to deal with it and make changes? I don't think so.

I will continue to have hope and pray for our leaders and all for all those who are suffering and will be suffering each day with addiction.

Definitions of the Different Programs When in Treatment and in the Court System

Outpatient:

Outpatient programs (OP) are for those seeking mental rehab or drug rehab, but who also stay at home every night. The main difference between outpatient treatment (OP) and intensive outpatient treatment (IOP) lies in the number of hours the patient spends at the facility. Most of the time, an outpatient program is designed for someone who has completed an inpatient stay and is looking to continue their growth in recovery. Outpatient is not meant to be the starting point; it is commonly referred to as aftercare.

Intensive Outpatient:

Intensive outpatient programs (IOP) are for those who want or need a very structured treatment program but who also wish to live at home and continue with certain responsibilities (such as work or school). IOP substance abuse treatment programs vary in duration and intensity, and certain outpatient rehab centers will offer individualized treatment programs.

Inpatient:

Residential treatment programs are those that offer housing and meals in addition to substance abuse treatment. Rehab facilities that offer residential treatment allow patients to focus solely on recovery in an environment totally separate from their lives. Some rehab centers specialize in short-term residential treatment (a few days to a week or two), while others solely provide treatment on a long-term basis (several weeks to months). Some offer both and tailor treatment to the patient's individual requirements.

Sober Living Homes:

Sober living houses (SLHs), a.k.a. sober homes or halfway houses, are safe, substance-free, supportive living facilities for those recovering from substance abuse. Ideal for those who've just been through inpatient or outpatient treatment, SLHs are supervised environments with rules that support sobriety, such as curfews, shared chores, and therapeutic meetings. Residents are also often trained on life skills and coping skills to make it easier to transition into society. SLHs also provide a strong sense of community that can lead to the kind of deep and lasting connections with other sober individuals that supports a new, healthy lifestyle.

Partial Hospitalization Program:

A partial hospitalization program (PHP) is a short-term form of intensive rehab, usually for those with acute symptoms that are hard to manage but don't require 24-hour care. PHPs have structured programming (i.e., individual and/or group therapy), and usually meet three to five days a week for around six hours (i.e. 9:00 AM to 3:00 PM). Some PHPs are residential (patients sleep on site), and some are not, so patients sleep at home. PHPs can last from one to six months, and some offer transportation and meals.

<u>New Jersey Court System</u>

Pretrial Intervention Program (PTI)

The pretrial intervention program is a program targeted at providing first-time offenders charged with non-violent crimes an opportunity to avoid the crippling consequences often associated with a felony criminal conviction. It also attempts to relieve some of the burden on the criminal justice system caused by such offenders. The program renders early rehabilitative services and aims to deter future criminal behavior. Many states have similar programs employed under a variety of names.